ASCENT®
CENTER FOR TECHNICAL KNOWLEDGE

Creo Parametric 2.0:
Introduction to Solid Modeling
Part 2

Student Guide

Revision 1.0
January 2013

ASCENT - Center for Technical Knowledge®
Creo Parametric 2.0
Introduction to Solid Modeling - Part 2
Revision 1.0

Prepared and produced by:

ASCENT Center for Technical Knowledge
630 Peter Jefferson Parkway, Suite 175
Charlottesville, VA 22911

866-527-2368
www.ASCENTed.com

ASCENT - Center for Technical Knowledge is a division of Rand Worldwide, Inc., providing custom developed knowledge products and services for leading engineering software applications. ASCENT is focused on specializing in the creation of education programs that incorporate the best of classroom learning and technology-based training offerings.

We welcome any comments you may have regarding this training guide, or any of our products. To contact us please email: feedback@ASCENTed.com.

General Disclaimer:

Notwithstanding any language to the contrary, nothing contained herein constitutes nor is intended to constitute an offer, inducement, promise, or contract of any kind. The data contained herein is for informational purposes only and is not represented to be error free. ASCENT, its agents and employees, expressly disclaim any liability for any damages, losses or other expenses arising in connection with the use of its materials or in connection with any failure of performance, error, omission even if ASCENT, or its representatives, are advised of the possibility of such damages, losses or other expenses. No consequential damages can be sought against ASCENT or Rand Worldwide, Inc. for the use of these materials by any third parties or for any direct or indirect result of that use.

The information contained herein is intended to be of general interest to you and is provided "as is", and it does not address the circumstances of any particular individual or entity. Nothing herein constitutes professional advice, nor does it constitute a comprehensive or complete statement of the issues discussed thereto. ASCENT does not warrant that the document or information will be error free or will meet any particular criteria of performance or quality. In particular (but without limitation) information may be rendered inaccurate by changes made to the subject of the materials (i.e. applicable software). Rand Worldwide, Inc. specifically disclaims any warranty, either expressed or implied, including the warranty of fitness for a particular purpose.

Table of Contents

Class Files

To download the Class Files that are required for this training guide, use the following steps:

1. Type the ftp address shown at the bottom of the page into the address bar of your internet browser. If you are using an ASCENT ebook you can select the link instead. The ftp address must be typed exactly as shown.

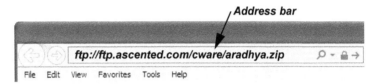

Address bar

2. Press <Enter> and follow the instructions to download the zip file that contains the Class Files.

3. The zip file contains an .exe file that you need to extract. To extract the files, double-click on the .exe file and follow the instructions to unzip the file. Once unzipped, a Class Files folder is automatically added to the C:\ drive on your computer.

   Do not change the location in which the Class Files folder is created. Doing so can prevent the practices in the training guide from working correctly.

ftp://ftp.ascented.com/cware/aradhya.zip

Chapter 15

Drawing Basics

Drawings can be created from the models created in Part or Assembly mode. Drawings are associative, so a change made in the model reflects in the drawing. As well, a change made in the drawing reflects in the model.

This chapter introduces:

> ✓**Creating a New Drawing**

Learning Objectives

This chapter provides instruction to enable you to do the following:

15.1 Creating a New Drawing

 Create a new drawing.

 Add General, Projected, Auxiliary, Detailed, and Section views to create the required documentation of a model.

 Show dimensions on a drawing using the Show Model Annotations dialog box.

 Create additional dimensions and notes in the drawing.

 Manipulate detail items using the contextual menu or the Properties dialog box.

15.1 Creating a New Drawing

 Create a new drawing.

 Add General, Projected, Auxiliary, Detailed, and Section views to create the required documentation of a model.

 Show dimensions on a drawing using the Show Model Annotations dialog box.

 Create additional dimensions and notes in the drawing.

 Manipulate detail items using the contextual menu or the Properties dialog box.

This section covers the process of creating a basic drawing of your model.

General Steps

Use the following general steps to create a drawing:

1. Create a new drawing.

2. Place the first drawing view.

3. Add views.

4. Modify view properties.

5. Manipulate drawing views, as needed.

6. Detail the drawing (e.g., dimensions, notes, tolerances, etc.).

7. Manipulate detail items, as needed.

8. Print (or Plot) the drawing.

Step 1 - Create a new drawing.

To create a new drawing, click ⬚ in the toolbar or select **File > New**. Select the **Drawing** option in the New dialog box, enter a name, and click OK . The New Drawing dialog box opens, as shown in Figure 15–1.

The default option in the Specify Template area is dependent on whether the **Use default template** option is selected in the New dialog box. If so, the **Use template** option is selected. If not the **Empty** option is selected.

Figure 15–1

The areas in the New Drawing dialog box are described in Table 15–1.

If a model is in session, Creo Parametric assigns that model as the default.

Table 15–1

Area	Description
Default Model	Enter the name or click **Browse...** to specify the model to be displayed in the drawing.
Specify Template	Select the **Use template**, **Empty with format**, or **Empty** option to specify whether you want to create the drawing with a predefined template, a format, or to leave the drawing empty.
Template	Enter the name or click **Browse...** to specify the template that is to be used in the drawing. Only available when the **Use template** option is selected.
Format	Enter the name or click **Browse...** to specify the format that is to be used in the drawing. Only available when the **Empty with format** option is selected.
Orientation and Size	Select the appropriate icon to define the orientation of the drawing sheet (portrait, landscape, or variable) and set the sheet size for the drawing. Only available when the **Empty** option is selected.

Templates

A drawing template contains predefined views, sets the view display, creates snap lines, and displays preassigned model dimensions based on the information specified when the template was created. Templates are discussed further in *Creo Parametric: Design Documentation & Detailing*.

Formats

A drawing format can contain standard information that is present in all drawings, such as the title block, company logo, BOM tables, etc. Drawing formats can be used in conjunction with drawing templates.

When you have finished making selections in the New Drawing dialog box, click **OK** to create the drawing.

Step 2 - Place the first drawing view.

Drawings created using a template already contain certain views. Additional views can be added at any time.

The first view placed on the drawing is always a General view. This kind of view is independent of other views. To place the first (General) view, right-click and select **Insert General View** or click

(General), in the Model Views group, in the *Layout* tab.

Select a location on the drawing to place the view. The General view is initially placed on the drawing sheet in its default orientation and the Drawing View dialog box opens, as shown in Figure 15–2.

Figure 15–2

By default, the *View Type* category settings are displayed in the Drawing View dialog box. You can enter the View name and change the default view orientation using the options in the *View orientation* area.

To modify the view orientation, you can select one the following methods in the *View orientation* area:

- View names from the model
- Geometry references
- Angles

To apply the new view orientation, click **Apply**.

View Names From the Model

The **View names from the model** option enables you to orient the General view on the drawing, using a predefined view saved from the model. The list of predefined views displays in the Drawing View dialog box, as shown in Figure 15–3.

Figure 15–3

Geometry References

The **Geometry references** option enables you to orient the General view using the orientation tools that are used in other 3D models. You must select an orientation (e.g., Front, Top, Right, etc.), and then select a planar surface, datum plane or coordinate system axis as its reference, as shown in Figure 15–4. The two references must be perpendicular to one another to orient the view into 2D.

Using default datum planes to orient the model is recommended. Orientation references can be lost if the selected planar surface references are later deleted.

Figure 15–4

You can click **Default orientation** to return the view to the default orientation.

Angles

The **Angles** option enables you to orient the General view by selecting a direction and entering angular values to place the view. The available directions are: Normal, Vertical, Horizontal, and Edge/Axis. The Normal, Vertical, and Horizontal directions are relative to the drawing sheet (monitor) and the Edge/Axis direction enables you to select a reference on the model from which to orient. Figure 15–5 shows the *Angles* area. You can add and remove orientation angles as needed, using ✛ and ▬.

Figure 15–5

For example, the model in Figure 15–6 is oriented to 2D using the **Geometry references** option and by selecting references for the **Front** and **Top** reference options.

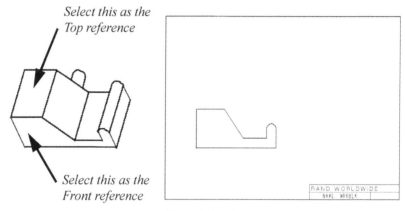

Select this as the Top reference

Select this as the Front reference

Figure 15–6

Once the orientation has been defined, click ^{OK} or ^{Close} in the Drawing View dialog box to continue the drawing creation.

Step 3 - Add views.

Additional view types are available after the first general view has been added. To place an additional view, click the icon representing the view you want use in the *Layout* tab, as shown in Figure 15-7.

Figure 15–7

Additional views and options for views can be found in the *Layout* tab.

The available view types are described in Table 15–2.

Table 15–2

Option	Description
General	A view that is originally displayed in 3D and can be oriented into 2D.
Projection	An orthographic projection of an existing view.
Detailed	A selected portion of an existing view.
Auxiliary	A view projected 90° to a surface, datum, or axis.
Revolved	A cross-section revolved 90° about a cut line.
Copy and Align	A copy of an existing Detailed view with a different boundary defined.

The available view types are dependent on the views that currently exist in the drawing, as well as whether a view is preselected before you select a view in the View toolbar. If a view is not selected, the system provides a more detailed list that enables you to create new parent views. If a view is preselected, the system assumes that you are creating a child view to the selected view and provides the appropriate view types. Figure 15–8 shows examples of different view types.

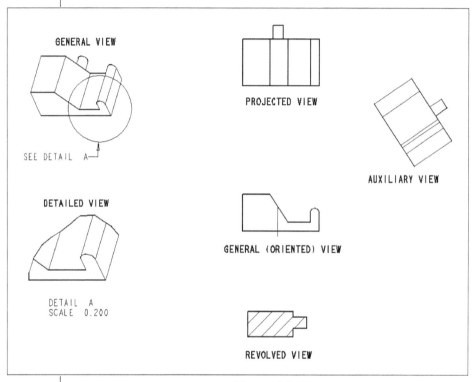

Figure 15–8

Shortcuts for General and Projected Views

To quickly create General, Projection, and Auxiliary views, you can right-click and select an option in the contextual menu. To create a General view, right-click and select **Insert General View** and place the view. To create a Projected or Auxiliary view, select the parent view, right-click, and select **Insert Projection View** or **Insert Auxiliary View.** Place the view relative to the parent view.

Step 4 - Modify view properties.

To change the view properties, double click on the view or select the view, right-click, and select **Properties**. The Drawing view dialog box opens. You can now change the properties in individual categories.

View Type

The *View Type* category enables you to change the view type in the Type drop-down list, as shown in Figure 15–9. For example, you can change the General view to a Projection view. Note that the view type modification can be restricted. Some view types might display in gray, indicating that they are not available for selection.

Figure 15–9

The *View Type* category enables you to change the view orientation, using the options in the *View orientation* area. See Step 1 for more detailed information.

When modifying a Detailed view, the *View Type* category enables you to re-sketch the view boundary. Select the *Reference point on parent view* collector and select the new reference point. Select the *Spline boundary on the parent view* collector and sketch the spline representing the view boundary. The options for the *View Type* category are shown in Figure 15–10.

Figure 15–10

Visible Area

The *Visible Area* category enables you to define the portion of the view (visibility) that is displayed, as well as view clipping options. The options are shown in Figure 15–11.

Figure 15–11

The visibility of a view can be defined as Full, Half, Partial, or Broken, as shown in Figure 15–12. Depending on the view type, some visibility options might not be available.

*The **Visible Area** options enable you to highlight key areas of a drawing view.*

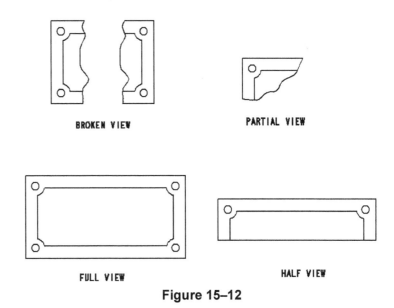

Figure 15–12

Scale

The *Scale* category enables you to define whether the view uses the default sheet scale (**Default scale for sheet**) or whether an independent scale is applied (**Custom scale**), as shown in Figure 15–13.

Figure 15–13

Default Scale for Sheet

Select the **Default scale for sheet** option in the Drawing View dialog box to set the default scale for a view. The default drawing scale displays in the lower left corner of the drawing, as shown in Figure 15–14. The scale value is based on sheet and model size, and affects all views in the drawing that are not independently scaled.

Figure 15–14

Custom Scale

Select the **Custom scale** option in the Drawing View dialog box to add an independent view scale. The scale value is displayed directly below the view, as shown in Figure 15–15. Customized scaling is useful when you want views to appear smaller or larger than the default scale permits.

*The scale values associated with individual views can be moved using the standard **Move** tools.*

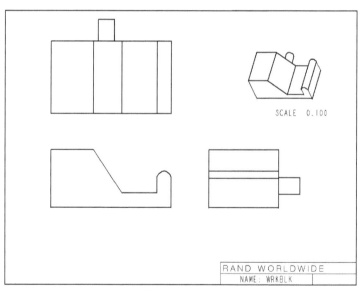

Figure 15–15

Sections

The *Sections* category enables you to define whether or not the view contains a cross-section. To add a 2D section created in the model while in Part mode, click ✚, select the cross-section name in the *Name* column, and select an area type in the *Sectioned Area* column, as shown in Figure 15–16. Click ▬ to remove a section from the view. Click ⤢ to flip the material side.

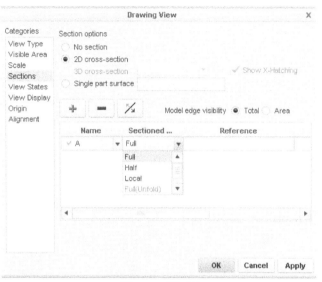

Figure 15–16

Figure 15–17 shows two of the basic cross-section types that can be used. These types are set using the **Model edge visibility** options.

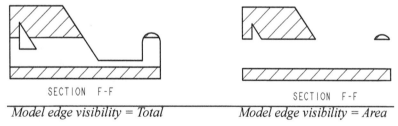

Model edge visibility = Total   *Model edge visibility = Area*

Figure 15–17

View Display

By default, all views are displayed according to the view display icon that is selected in the toolbar (⬚ (Wireframe), ⬚ (No Hidden), ⬚ (Hidden Line), or ⬚ (Shading)). This setting affects all views in the drawing. The *View Display* category enables you to set the display for each view using the Display style drop-down list as shown in Figure 15–18. Once set, the display for the view is independent of the settings made in the Creo Parametric session.

Figure 15–18

Step 5 - Manipulate drawing views, as needed.

Once views have been added and modified, some common changes can be made to them including: deleting views, moving views, changing scale, and view display.

Delete Views

Deleted views are permanently removed from the drawing.

Views can be deleted from a drawing using any of the following methods.

* Select the view, right-click, and select **Delete**.
* Select the view and press <Delete>.
* Select the view and click ✕ in the *Annotate* tab.
* Select the view name in the Drawing tree, right-click and select **Delete**.

Move Views

Views are automatically locked to the original location at which they were placed. To enable movement of views, clear the checkmark next to **Lock View Movement** in the contextual menu or click ⬛⮕ (Lock View Movement) in the Document group in the *Layout* tab. Once unlocked, you can select the view and drag it as needed on the drawing. All dependent views move relative to their parents. Once you finish moving a view, it is recommended that you relock the view movement using the same tool.

Change Scale

To modify the default drawing scale, double-click on the scale value in the lower left corner of the drawing and enter a value at the prompt. Changing this value affects the scale of all but the independently scaled views.

To modify the scale of an independently scaled view, select the note containing the scale value, and double-click on the scale value inside the note. You can also select the note containing the scale value. Select the scale value, right-click, and select **Edit Value**.

Step 6 - Detail the drawing (e.g., dimensions, notes, tolerances, etc.).

When drawing views have been placed on a drawing, you can add dimensions and notes to communicate information to manufacturing. These items are associative and update with changes to other views and modifications to the model. Detail items display in the drawing tree as shown in Figure 15–19.

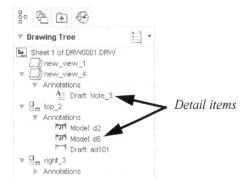

Figure 15–19

Dimensions

Dimensions can be shown or created to provide the required dimensional information for manufacturing the model, as shown in Figure 15–20.

Dimensions can be created in Drawing mode, but these dimensions do not drive the geometry. Only those displayed directly from the model can drive the geometry.

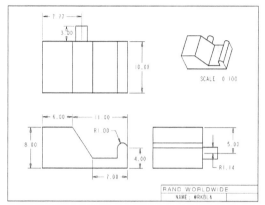

Figure 15–20

Showing Model Annotations

Model dimensions refer to dimensions that are used to create the part model.

Use the following steps to display or erase model dimensions:

1. Select the *Annotate* tab.

*Dimensions can also be added by selecting a feature in the model tree, right-clicking and selecting **Show Model Annotation**.*

2. Click (Show Model Annotations) in the Annotations group or right-click on the feature in the model tree and select **Show Model Annotations**. The Show Model Annotations dialog box opens as shown in Figure 15–21.

Figure 15–21

3. Select the *Dimension* tab (⊢⊣). Expand the Type drop-down list and select **All** as the type of dimension as shown in Figure 15–22.

Figure 15–22

4. Select a feature in the view in which you want the dimensions to display in the drawing window. The dimensions display on the view in red and in the dialog box. Select the dimensions that you want to keep for that view as shown in Figure 15–23. They display in black. Use <Ctrl> to select multiple features or views.

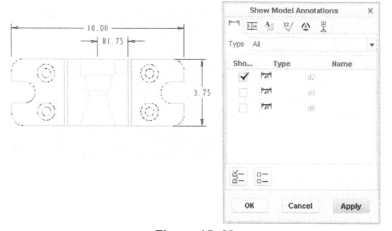

Figure 15–23

5. Click **Apply** .

6. Repeat the procedure to add dimensions to other features in the drawing.

Table 15–3 describes additional detail items that can be added to a drawing.

Table 15–3

Icon	Description	Icon	Description
⊢──┤	Dimension	ⒶⒶ	Symbol
⌖ⓜ	Geometric Tolerance	32/	Surface Finish
A⁼	Note	🔺	Datum Plane

Creating Dimensions

When showing dimensions, only those that were created in the model are displayed. If a required dimension does not exist in the model (and therefore is not shown), it can be created. Since created dimensions are driven by the model geometry, their values cannot be modified. However, these values automatically update if the geometry changes in the part. Only displayed dimension values can be modified to change the model.

To create a dimension, click ⊢──┤ in the *Annotate* tab. Select the references on the drawing view and place the dimension with the middle mouse button. Dimensions created in Drawing mode use the same creation methods as in Sketcher mode.

Notes

Notes can be added to detail the drawing, as shown in Figure 15–24.

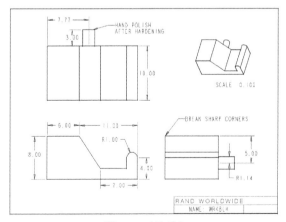

Figure 15–24

Click ⁴≡ in the *Annotation* tab to start the creation of a note. The **NOTE TYPES** menu displays, enabling you to define how the note is added to the drawing. You can customize the following:

- How the leader for the note is displayed (e.g., no leader, leader, or ISO leader).
- How the text for the note is entered (e.g., entered at a prompt or read from a file).
- How the text is displayed (e.g., horizontal or vertical).
- How the text is justified (e.g., left, center, or right).

Once the options in the **NOTE TYPES** menu are defined, select **Make Note** to create the note. Instructions are displayed in the message window as you create and place the note.

Notes can incorporate parametric information that updates as the model changes. An ampersand (&) symbol is used to incorporate parametric information. For example, the parametric note shown in Figure 15–25 is entered as [&d23 DRILL- &P0 HOLES], where the &d23 and &P0 reference dimension values are from the model. When you include parametric information, modifications to the size or number of holes in the pattern automatically update in the note.

During note creation, dimensions are displayed in their symbolic form.

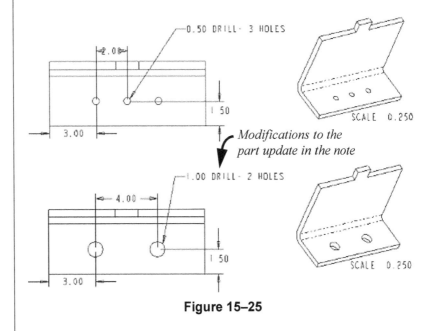

Figure 15–25

Step 7 - Manipulate detail items, as needed.

Once detail items have been added to a drawing, changes might be required. Some common changes that can be made to detail items include moving detail items, erasing, editing values, flipping arrows, moving an item to a view, and adding dimensional tolerances.

Move Detail Items

Select and drag detail items to move them, as needed.

Erase

You can erase detail items by selecting the item in the drawing, right-clicking, and selecting **Erase**. The erased annotations still display in the drawing tree as shown in Figure 15–26.

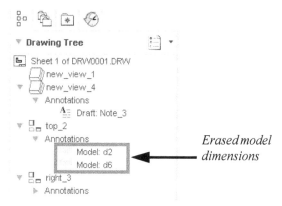

Figure 15–26

Edit Values

The value for a model dimension can be modified directly in Drawing mode. The change is reflected in the model. To modify a dimension value, select the dimension, right-click, and select **Properties**. Another way to modify a dimension is to double-click on the value. Created dimensions cannot be modified. However, changes to the model geometry are reflected in the updated dimension value.

Flip Arrows

Right-click and select **Flip Arrows** to change the direction of the dimension arrows.

Move Item to View

When detail items, such as dimensions, are displayed on the drawing, they are not necessarily displayed on the required view. To switch detail items between views, select the dimension(s), right-click, and select **Move Item to View** as shown in Figure 15–27. Select the new view on which you want the dimension to be displayed. You can select multiple items to be moved by pressing and holding down <Ctrl> as you are selecting them.

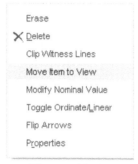

Figure 15–27

Dimensional Tolerances

To enable dimension tolerances in Drawing mode, the Drawing Options file must have the **tol_display** option set to **yes**. To open the Options dialog box and set the value, select **File > Prepare > Drawing Properties**. The Drawing Properties dialog box opens as shown in Figure 15–28. Select **change** in the *Detail Options* area.

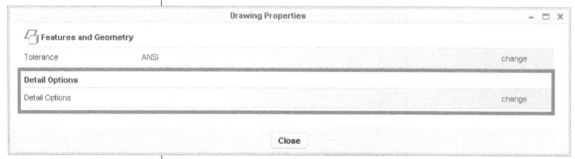

Figure 15–28

To set dimension tolerances, select the dimension(s), right-click, and select **Properties**. You can also double-click on the dimension. The Dimension Properties dialog box opens, as shown in Figure 15–29.

Figure 15–29

The available tolerance modes are listed in Table 15–4.

Table 15–4

Option	Example
Nominal	1.25
+/- Symmetric	1.25 ± 0.05
Plus-Minus	1.25 $^{+0.05}_{-0.01}$
Limits	1.30 1.20

Step 8 - Print (or Plot) the drawing.

To print or plot the drawing, select **File > Print > Print**. The Print dialog box opens displaying all of the plotting options, as shown in Figure 15–30.

Figure 15–30

To print the file, you must define the destination printer in the drop-down list and configure it, as needed. You must also select whether the file is printed to the printer or to a file and the number of copies.

Exercise 15a | Create a Drawing

 Create a new drawing based on a drawing template.

 Add General, Projected, Section, and Detail views to create a drawing.

 Change the orientation, display style, scale, and add a section using the View dialog box.

 Show dimensions on the drawing using the Show Model Annotations dialog box.

 Create and edit notes in the drawing.

In this exercise, you will create the drawing shown in Figure 15–31, using a predefined format. To complete the drawing, add all of the necessary views, dimensions, and notes. Manipulate them as needed to match the detail shown in Figure 15–31.

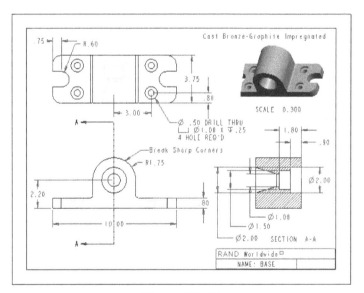

Figure 15–31

Goal | After you complete this exercise, you will be able to:

✓ Place and manipulate drawing views

✓ **Show and manipulate drawing dimensions**
✓ **Create notes on a drawing**

Task 1 - Create a drawing and open a format.

1. Set the working directory to the *exercise 15a* folder.

2. Click .

3. In the *Type* area in the New dialog box, select the **Drawing** option.

4. For the drawing name, enter [base].

5. Clear the **Use default template** option to create the drawing without a template.

6. Click OK.

7. Click Browse... and browse to and select **base.prt**.

8. In the *Specify Template* area in the New Drawing dialog box, select the **Empty with format** option.

9. In the *Format* area, click Browse... , browse to the working directory, and select the **rand.frm** format file as shown in Figure 15–32.

Figure 15–32

10. Click **OK** to finish creating the drawing. A drawing sheet is displayed in the main window

11. Select **File > Prepare > Drawing Properties**. Select **change** in the *Detail Options* area as shown in Figure 15–33.

Figure 15–33

12. In the Option panel, enter [tol_display]. In the value field, set the *Value* to **No**. Add the change and close the dialog box. Close the Drawing Properties dialog box.

Task 2 - Add four views to the drawing.

In this task you will create the views shown in Figure 15–34.

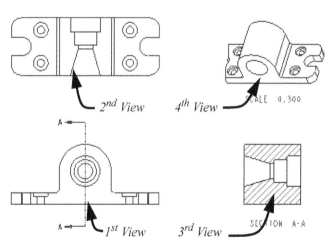

Figure 15–34

1. Change the display style to wireframe.

2. Verify that the *Layout* tab is selected. Click 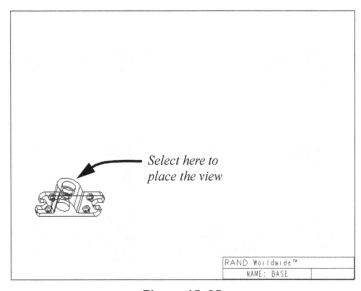 (General) to add the first view. You can also right-click and select **Insert General View**.

3. If the Select Combine State dialog box opens, select **Do not prompt for Combine State** and click the **OK** button. Select a location on the screen to place the first General view, as shown in Figure 15–35.

Select here to place the view

RAND Worldwide™
NAME: BASE

Figure 15–35

*To reorient the model, you can also select the **Geometry references** option and select two orthogonal planar references. Use the default datum planes for the orientation references.*

4. Orient the view, as shown in Figure 15–37. In the Drawing View dialog box, the **View names from the model** option is selected, enabling you to select a predefined model view to orient the model. In the *Model view names* area, double-click on the FRONT view to reorient the model, as shown in Figure 15–36.

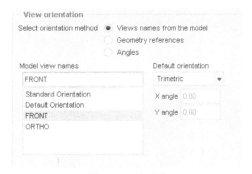

Figure 15–36

5. Click **OK** to complete the view placement. The view displays as shown in Figure 15–37.

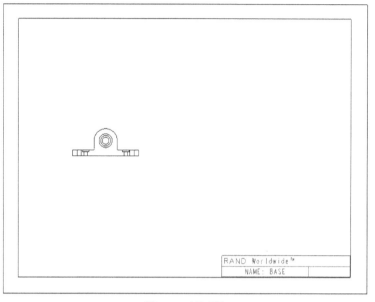

Figure 15–37

You can also click

(Projection).

A Projected view cannot have an independent scale. It must have the same scale as its parent General view.

6. Select the first view, right-click, and select **Insert Projection View**. Place the second view at the location shown in Figure 15–38.

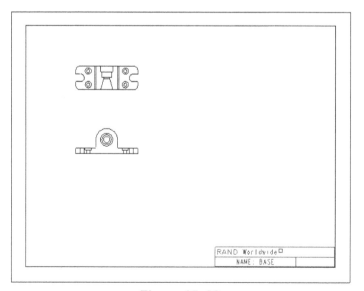

Figure 15–38

7. Select the first view, right-click, and select **Projection** or click  (Projection). Place the third view in the location shown in Figure 15–39.

Figure 15–39

You can also open the Drawing View dialog box by double-clicking on the view.

8. Select the third view, right-click, and select **Properties**.

9. In the Drawing View dialog box, select the *Sections* category.

10. In the *Section options* area, select the **2D cross-sections** option. Click ✛.

11. In the *Name* column, select cross-section **A**. In the *Sectioned Area* column, select the **Full** option as shown in Figure 15–40.

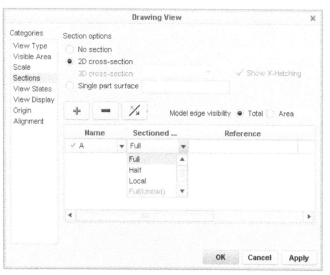

Figure 15–40

12. Click **OK** to complete the view modification.

13. Select the third view, right-click, and select **Add Arrows**. Select the first view in which to place cross-section arrows. The third view displays as shown in Figure 15–41.

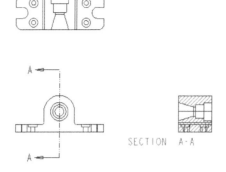

Figure 15–41

14. Click the **General View** icon and add the fourth view, as shown in Figure 15–42. Keep the View dialog box open. You can also right-click and select **Insert General View**.

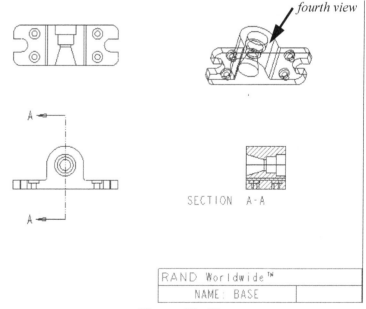

Figure 15–42

15. In the Drawing View dialog box, select the *Visible Area* category.

16. In the View Visibility drop-down list, select **Partial View**.

17. Select the edge in the fourth view as shown in Figure 15–43, to specify the reference point of the partial view. The cross symbol displays in the view.

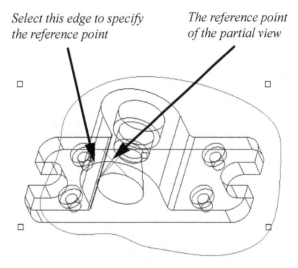

Select this edge to specify the reference point

The reference point of the partial view

Figure 15–43

18. Sketch a spline around the area to be displayed in the partial view as shown in Figure 15–43. Start sketching the spline at a suitable location. Define the internal points by clicking the left mouse button several times to create the spline by blending all of the selected points together. Complete the spline by pressing the middle mouse button.

19. Click **Apply** to apply the changes.

20. In the Drawing View dialog box, select the *Scale* category.

21. In the *Scale and perspective options* area, select the **Custom scale** option. For the scale, enter [0.3].

22. Click **Apply** to apply the changes.

23. Click **Close** to close the Drawing View dialog box. The fourth view displays as shown in Figure 15–44.

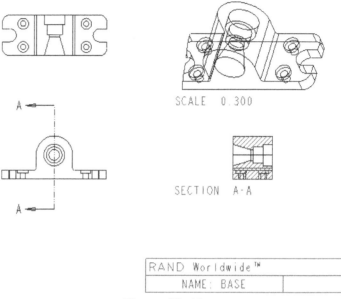

SCALE 0.300

SECTION A-A

RAND Worldwide™
NAME: BASE

Figure 15–44

Task 3 - Modify the scale of the drawing and move the views.

1. Double-click on the scale value in the lower left corner of the drawing and enter the scale value in the message window, as shown in Figure 15–45.

Enter value for scale

0.400

SCALE :0.400 TYPE :PART NAME :BASE SIZE :C

Sheet 1

Figure 15–45

2. Enter [0.4]. The scale of the fourth view remains set at **0.3** because this view has a scale that is independent to the rest of the drawing.

You can also click

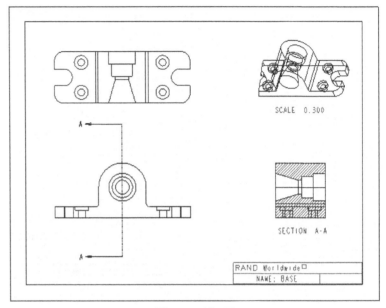

(Lock View Movement) in the Document group in the Layout tab to lock and unlock all of the views.

3. You can lock or unlock views to prevent them being moved by the mouse. To unlock them, select a view, right-click, and ensure the checkmark is cleared next to **Lock View Movement.** This enables movement.

4. Select the views individually and move them, as shown in Figure 15–46. Note how moving a parent view reflects in the placement of dependent views.

Figure 15–46

Task 4 - Change the view display of the third and fourth views.

*You can modify the view display for multiple views at the same time. Press and hold down <Ctrl> while selecting the views, right-click, and select **Properties** to open the Drawing View dialog box.*

1. Change the view display to **Hidden Line** in the Graphics toolbar.

2. Double-click on the third view.

3. In the Drawing View dialog box, select the *View Display* category.

4. In the Display Style drop-down list, select **No Hidden**.

5. Click OK to complete the view modification.

6. Repeat Steps 1 to 4 for the fourth view. The drawing displays as shown in Figure 15–47.

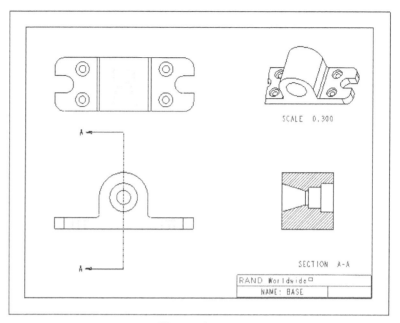

Figure 15–47

Task 5 - Change the view display of the fourth view.

1. Double-click on the fourth view.

2. In the Drawing View dialog box, select the *View Display* category.

3. In the Display Style drop-down list, select **Shading**.

4. Click OK to complete the view modification. The drawing displays as shown in Figure 15–48.

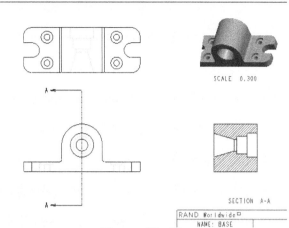

Figure 15–48

Task 6 - Display the dimensions of the base feature.

You can also use the model tree to display dimensions for each feature.

1. Select the *Annotate* tab. Click ![icon] (Show Model Annotations) to open the Show Model Annotations dialog box.

2. Select the *Dimensions* tab (![icon]). Verify that the **All** type is selected.

3. In the Top view, select the base feature **(F5(PROTRUSION))**.

4. Three dimensions display. In the *Show* column, place a check next to the 3.75 dimension (d0), and click **Apply**, as shown in Figure 15–49.

Figure 15–49

5. In the Front view, select the base feature **(F5(PROTRUSION))**.

   Keep the dimensions shown in Figure 15–50. Click **Apply** .

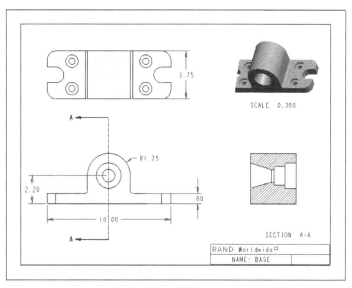

Figure 15–50

Task 7 - Display the dimensions of the U-shaped cut and the hole in the boss.

---

1. Display and select the dimensions of the U-shaped cut, as shown in Figure 15–51. If the cut was copied, you must select the original cut, which is on the left side of the view.

Select this cut

Show these dimensions

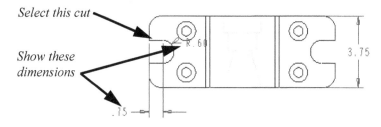

Figure 15–51

2. Click **Apply** in the Show Model Annotations dialog box to keep the dimensions.

3. Display the dimensions for the hole in the boss F19 (CUT) by selecting the feature on the Right (cross-section) view, as shown in Figure 15–52. Click ⌧– to select all the dimensions. If selecting the hole in the first or third view, right-click and select **Pick From List**. If required, you can change the default locations of the dimensions.

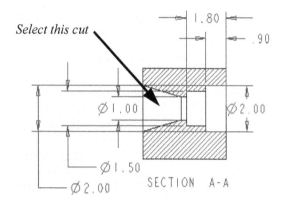

Figure 15–52

4. Click Apply in the Show Model Annotations dialog box to keep the dimensions.

5. Click Cancel to close the Show Model Annotations dialog box.

Task 8 - Delete dimensions.

1. Select any unwanted dimensions, right-click, and select **Delete** to remove them. Repaint the screen if necessary.

Task 9 - Continue selecting features to show dimensions.

1. Show dimensions for the remaining features.

2. When all of the dimensions are displayed, close the Show Model Annotations dialog box.

Task 10 - Arrange the dimensions.

1. Select one of the hole dimensions in the Top view, right-click once to flip the arrows, and move the dimension to the location shown in Figure 15–53.

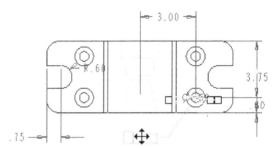

Figure 15–53

2. Select the **2.00** diameter dimension on the Section view, right-click, and select **Move Item To View**. Select the Top view. The dimension displays as shown in Figure 15–54.

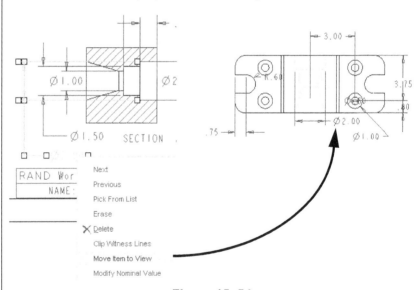

Figure 15–54

3. Undo the previous step.

4. Use the options in the toolbar or right-click and select an option to rearrange the locations of the dimensions, as shown in Figure 15–55.

Model dimensions can only be shown once on a drawing.

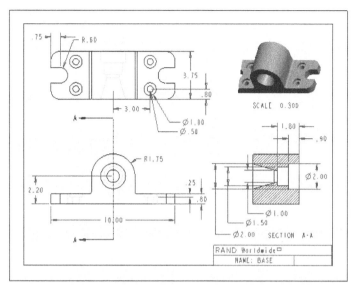

Figure 15–55

Task 11 - Create additional dimensions.

Dimensions are created similar to sketcher dimensions. Created dimensions update with any part changes. However, they cannot be modified to drive part geometry.

1. Click ⊢⊣. The Menu Manager opens. Leave the default options selected.

2. Create some dimensions in the drawing by selecting the entities with the left mouse button and then clicking the middle mouse button to place the dimension. This is similar to creating sketcher dimensions.

Task 12 - Delete some dimensions.

*Alternatively, right-click, and select **Delete**.*

1. Select any of the created dimensions and click ✗ or press <Delete>.

Task 13 - Create Note A.

In this task, you will create the three notes shown in Figure 15–56.

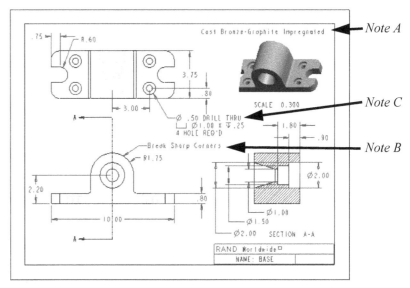

Figure 15–56

1. Select the *Annotation* tab and click ![icon] to create the first note.

When you select a location for a note, the dimensions change to their symbolic format.

2. Define the type of note by selecting **No Leader > Enter > Horizontal > Standard > Default > Make Note**.

3. Select a location at which to place the note, as shown in Figure 15–56.

4. Enter [Cast Bronze-Graphite Impregnated].

5. Press <Enter> to complete the note, and press <Enter> again to finish adding lines to the note.

Task 14 - Create Note B.

1. Select **With Leader** and accept the remaining defaults. Select **Make Note**.

2. Select **On Entity > Arrowhead** to define the type of attachment for the leader.

3. Read the message window and select the boss edge, as shown in Figure 15–56.

4. Click OK and select **Done**.

5. Select a location to place the note.

6. For the note, enter [Break Sharp Corners].

7. Press <Enter> twice to finish creating the note.

Task 15 - Create Note C.

---

1. Select **Make Note** to accept the **NOTE TYPE** menu defaults.

2. Select any of the counterbore holes.

3. Click OK and select **Done**.

4. Select a location at which to place the note.

As symbols are selected in the palette, they display in the message window.

5. Enter the note shown in Figure 15–57. In the palette window, select all of the special symbols except the ampersand (&) symbol. Use the keyboard to enter the ampersand symbol. Place the cursor in the *Prompt* area and continue to enter the note. Press <Enter> once after you complete each of the first two lines, and twice after the third line.

$$\varnothing \& d68 \ DRILL \ THRU$$
$$\sqcup \varnothing \& d67 \ X \ \nabla \& d66$$
$$4 \ HOLE \ REQ'D$$

Figure 15–57

6. Select **Done/Return**.

Task 16 - Modify Note A.

---

1. Select **Note A**, right-click, and select **Properties**.

2. The Note Properties dialog box opens, in which you can modify and edit the text for the note. Edit the note to span two lines.

3. Click **OK** to close the Note Properties dialog box and update the note.

Task 17 - Move the notes and save the drawing.

1. Move the notes by selecting them and dragging them to a new location.

2. Select a note and drag the leader to relocate it.

3. Save the drawing and erase all of the files from memory.

Exercise 15b | Create a Drawing using Additional Tools

 Create a new drawing, add views, and show dimensions.

In this exercise, you will use drawing tools to create the drawing shown in Figure 15–59. Tips are provided for you to create the radial circle of dimensions for the pattern of holes.

Goal

After you complete this exercise, you will be able to:

✓ **Create a drawing**
✓ **Detail a radial circle for patterned holes**

Task 1 - Open a part file.

---

1. Set the working directory to the *exercise 15b* folder.

2. Open **end_cap.prt**. The part displays as shown in Figure 15–58.

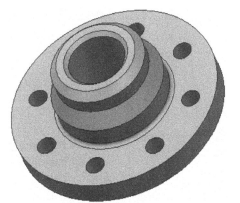

Figure 15–58

3. Review the part and its features.

Task 2 - Create a drawing with limited instruction.

1. Create the drawing shown in Figure 15–59.

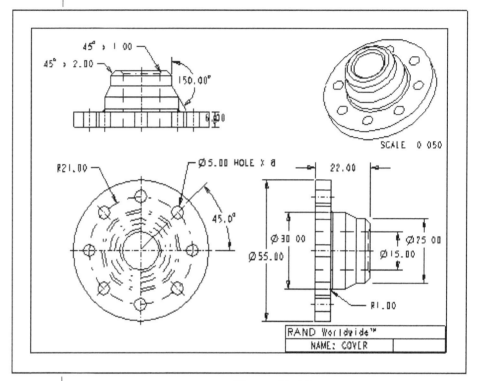

Figure 15–59

Use the following information to help you create the radial circle for the pattern:

* In the drawing setup file, edit an option. Select **File > Prepare > Drawing Options** and select **change** in the Detail Options dialog box. Edit the **radial_pattern_axis_circle** option, and set the option to **Yes**.
* Select the view, right-click and select **Show Model Annotation**.

2. Save the drawing and erase the files from memory.

Review Questions

1. Which of the following **Specify Template** options enables you to define the orientation of the drawing sheet and set the sheet size for the drawing?

   a. Use template

   b. Empty with format

   c. Empty

2. Which of the following view types must be the first view in a drawing?

   a. Projection

   b. Auxiliary

   c. General

   d. Detailed

3. Which of the following view types enables you to create a 3D view in its default orientation?

   a. Projection

   b. Auxiliary

   c. General

   d. Detailed

4. An independent view scale enables you to ensure that a view maintains the same scale value as the drawing.

   a. True

   b. False

5. Which of the following references can be selected when orienting a view? (Select all that apply.)

   a. Datum planes

   b. Datum axis

   c. Planar surfaces

   d. Cylindrical surfaces

   e. Coordinate system axis

6. Views are automatically locked to the original location at which they were placed. Which of the following options or icons enables you to unlock the view movement?

   a. Click ⊢─⊣ in the toolbar.

   b. Click ⁄ in the toolbar.

   c. Right-click and select **Unlock**.

   d. Right-click and select **Lock View Movement** to clear the checkmark next to the option.

7. Which of the following categories in the Drawing View dialog box enables you to redefine a Projected view as a General view?

   a. View Type

   b. Visible Area

   c. Sections

   d. View Display

8. Which of the following options enables you to display a dimension? (Select all that apply.)

   a. Click ⊢─⊣ .

   b. Right-click on the feature in the tree and select **Show Model Annotation**.

   c. Select the *Layout* tab.

   d. Click ⧓M.

9. Which of the following icons enables you to display model dimensions in a drawing?

   a. �

   b. ⊢─⊣

   c. A≡

   d. ⟨A⟩

10. To modify a created dimension value, select the dimension and right-click and select **Properties**.

   a. True

   b. False

Command Summary

Button	Command	Location
	General View	• **Ribbon:** *Layout* tab in the *Model Views* group • **Contextual menu:** Nothing selected
	Projection	• **Ribbon:** *Layout* tab in the *Model Views* group • **Contextual menu:** Select a view
	Detailed	• **Ribbon:** *Layout* tab in the *Model Views* group • **Contextual menu:** Nothing selected
	Show Model Annotations	• **Ribbon:** *Annotate* tab in the *Annotate* group • **Contextual Menu:** Select a feature or view in model or model tree
	Dimension	• **Ribbon:** *Annotate* tab in the *Annotate* group • **Contextual menu:** Nothing selected
	Note	• **Ribbon:** *Annotate* tab in the *Annotate* group
	Lock View Movement	• **Ribbon:** *Layout* tab in the *Document* group • **Contextual menu:** Select a view

Chapter 16

Parent/Child Relationships

Parent/child relationships are defined as a dependency between features. They are established as you add each additional feature to the model. If the parent feature is modified or deleted, the child feature(s) are affected. Parent/child relationships are a very powerful aspect of Creo Parametric. This chapter covers methods for controlling parent/child relationships to use them to your advantage.

This chapter introduces:

- ✓ **Establishing Parent/Child Relationships**
- ✓ **Controlling Parent/Child Relationships**
- ✓ **Investigating Parent/Child Relationships**
- ✓ **Changing Parent/Child Relationships**

Learning Objectives

This chapter provides instruction to enable you to do the following:

16.1 Establishing Parent/Child Relationships

 Understand the parent/child relationships that are established when creating pick and place features.

 Understand the parent/child relationships that are established when creating sketched features.

16.2 Controlling Parent/Child Relationships

 Understand how parent/child relationships are established between features and how to best control them.

16.3 Investigating Parent/Child Relationships

 Recognize the possible relationships between features in the model using the model tree or model player.

 Identify all equations that have been established in a model using the Relations or Parameters dialog box.

 Identify relationships between features in the model using the commands in the *Tools* tab.

16.4 Changing Parent/Child Relationships

 Change an existing parent/child relationship in a model using the editing tools.

16.1 Establishing Parent/Child Relationships

 Understand the parent/child relationships that are established when creating pick and place features.

 Understand the parent/child relationships that are established when creating sketched features.

Parent/child relationships are created as a result of dependency between features. The independent feature is referred to as the parent and the dependent feature is the child. When such a dependency exists, Creo Parametric uses the parent feature to place or locate the child feature. Parent/child relationships can be created when either pick and place or sketched features are used.

Pick and Place Features

The shape of pick and place features (e.g., holes, rounds, or chamfers) is predefined. Therefore, you are not required to sketch the section. You only need to select the placement references to locate the feature on the model. The placement references that you select establish parent/child relationships between the new feature and the existing features that were used for placement. The hole in the model shown on the right in Figure 16–1 is created as a coaxial hole. The placement references establish the parent/child relationships.

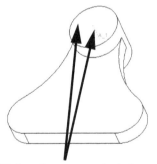 

Hole references: axis A_1 and the planar surface of the cylindrical protrusion

The hole is a child of this protrusion

Figure 16–1

The round in the model shown on the right side in Figure 16–2 is created by referencing the indicated edge. The edge reference establishes a parent/child relationship with a previous protrusion.

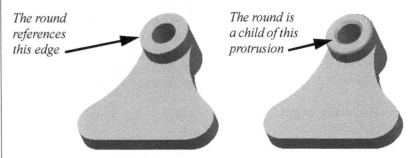

The round references this edge

The round is a child of this protrusion

Figure 16–2

The chamfer in the model shown on the right in Figure 16–3 is created by referencing the indicated edge. The edge reference establishes a parent/child relationship with the previous protrusion.

The chamfer references this edge

The chamfer is a child of the hole

Figure 16–3

Sketched Features

The process of creating a sketched feature results in the creation of parent/child relationships. Relationships are established for the following:

- Sketching and orientation plane references
- Section selection
- Sketching References
- Depth options

Sketching and Orientation Plane References

The sketch plane defines a planar reference on which a 2D section is sketched. The orientation plane defines the reference required to orient the sketch plane for sketching. The sketch and orientation references are then established as parents of the sketched feature.

If the sketch or orientation reference is created during the creation of the feature, the references used to create the required reference also establish a parent/child relationship.

In Figure 16–4, the sketch plane for a new sketched feature is a surface belonging to a protrusion. This makes the new feature a child of the protrusion. The sketch orientation reference is datum plane FRONT. This makes the new feature a child of datum plane FRONT. The Section dialog box shown in Figure 16–4 displays the references that were selected for the sketch.

*Creo Parametric might select an orientation reference plane by default. If this reference does not provide the required parent/child relationship, you can create a new one by selecting the Reference text field in the dialog box and selecting the new reference in the model. You can also change the **Orientation** option.*

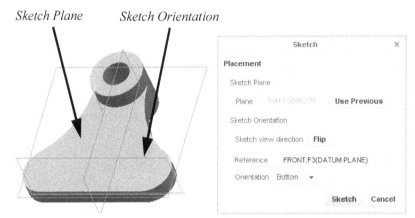

Sketch Plane   *Sketch Orientation*

Figure 16–4

Section Selection

The section for a sketched feature can be sketched within the feature, or you can select an existing sketch in the model to reference. If an existing sketch is selected, it is copied into the current sketch and maintains an associative link to the original sketch. This establishes a parent/child relationship between the sketch and the sketched feature. Any changes to the sketch are reflected in the solid geometry.

Sketching References

Sketching references, such as entities, model edges, surfaces, and features are used to locate sketched geometry. When you select sketching references, parent/child relationships are established. The sketched geometry is located with respect to these entities using dimensions and constraints.

To review sketcher

references, click 🔲
*while you are in the
Sketch tab.*

*Sketching references
display in the sketch as
cyan dashed lines.*

Sketching references are provided in the References dialog box as shown in Figure 16–5. The default references include a horizontal and vertical datum plane for locating the sketch on the model. These references create a parent/child relationship with the datum features.

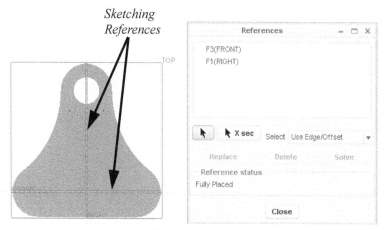

Figure 16–5

The default references might not provide you with the references you need to meet your design intent. Additional references, such as edges, surfaces, axes, or coordinate systems can also be selected to establish parent/child relationships.

In Figure 16–6, the cut is located by selecting the surface of the square protrusion as a reference and sketching the cut using the point on entity constraint. The reference between the two ensures that the cut is a child of the protrusion and that they always remain in alignment.

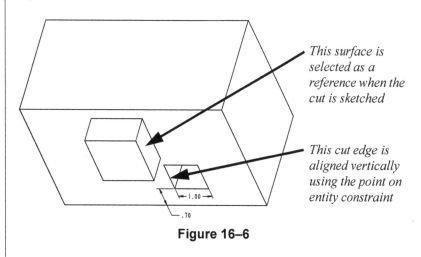

Figure 16–6

In Figure 16–7, the square cut was located by dimensioning it to the hole and the chamfer. The cut is now a child of both the hole and the chamfer.

It is not recommended that you dimension a feature to another feature that could change later in the design (e.g., rounds or chamfers). If the reference feature is changed or deleted the new feature can no longer be positioned properly or might lose its reference and fail.

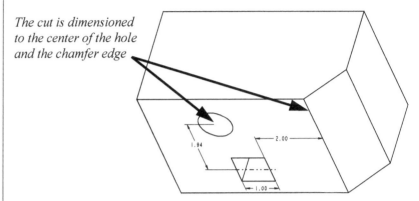

The cut is dimensioned to the center of the hole and the chamfer edge

Figure 16–7

Certain geometry creation operations, such as projecting or offsetting an existing edge, create an implicit alignment and therefore establish parent/child relationships. In Figure 16–8, the entities at the bottom of the base protrusion are selected as edge references for offsetting. The new feature is a child of the base feature. Once the sketching references have been selected for offsetting, they are automatically added to the References dialog box.

A parent/child relationship would have also been established if concentric arcs were used to create the feature.

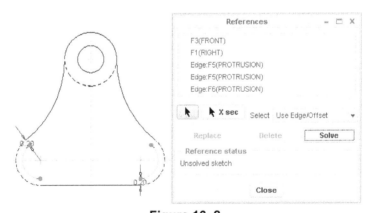

Figure 16–8

If you select a sketcher reference and it is not used (i.e., geometry is not located with respect to the reference with either a dimension or constraint), the reference is deleted when the sketch is complete and a parent/child relationship is not established.

Depth Options

It is recommended that you select surfaces instead of edges as references because an edge is more likely to change than a surface.

Some **Depth** options establish parent/child relationships. These options, as shown in Figure 16–9, establish parent/child relationships because a point, curve, plane, or surface is required as a reference to define the depth. These options include the following:

- **Extrude to Selected Point, Curve, Plane, or Surface**
- **Extrude to Intersect with selected Surface or Plane**

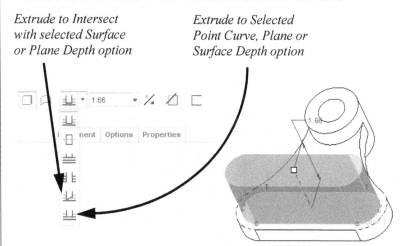

Extrude to Intersect with selected Surface or Plane Depth option

Extrude to Selected Point Curve, Plane or Surface Depth option

Figure 16–9

16.2 Controlling Parent/Child Relationships

 Understand how parent/child relationships are established between features and how to best control them.

Parent/child relationships can make models more robust and powerful. Use the following tips for controlling parent/child relationships:

- Create and use default datum planes. Since these are never deleted, they are useful as sketching and orientation plane selections. This establishes the datums, rather than a geometric feature, as parents of the sketched feature.
- Think about the surface you are selecting as a sketching or reference plane. Is this surface the best selection as a parent for this feature?
- When in the *Sketch* tab, select references with the model in a 3D orientation to ensure that you are selecting the proper references (i.e. surfaces, not edges).
- Use the hidden feature selection techniques to identify what is being selected. The help line describes the selected entity and the system highlights the reference and displays a message.
- When in the *Sketch* tab, consider the references used with tools such as project and offsetting edges as well as sketching concentric arcs and circles.
- Think about the references (points, curves, planes, or surfaces) that you are selecting when using the **Extrude to Selected Point, Curve, Plane or Surface** and **Extrude to Intersect with selected Surface or Plane Depth** options. Is this reference the best selection of a parent for this feature?
- Once a pick and place or sketched feature has been created you can also establish a parent/child relationship using relations. It is good practice to ensure that all of the relations contain a comment statement explaining the purpose of the relation.

16.3 Investigating Parent/Child Relationships

 Recognize the possible relationships between features in the model using the model tree or model player.

 Identify all equations that have been established in a model using the Relations or Parameters dialog box.

 Identify relationships between features in the model using the commands in the *Tools* tab.

It is not practical to assume that you are always creating new models. In many cases you are required to continue someone else's design or make modifications to a previously completed model. In these cases, always investigate the model to understand the existing design and parent/child relationships. You can use the following review techniques:

- Model tree
- Relations
- Tools tab
- Model player

Model Tree

The model tree displays all of the features in the model. By reviewing the model tree you can understand the hierarchy of the model and understand which feature can reference others.

Show Relations

Relations are used in models to control the design intent. In doing so, they establish parent/child relationships. To investigate existing relations in a model, select the *Tools* tab > **Model Intent > Relations and Parameters**. Any existing relations display in the viewer. You can also click $d=$ (Relations) in the *Tools* tab and click |↔| to review which dimensions are affected by the relation.

Tools tab

(Model) in the *Tools* tab, is used to obtain model information as shown in Figure 16–10.

Model Info : BRACKET

PART NAME :	BRACKET					
Units:		Length:	Mass:	Force:	Time:	Temperature:
Inch lbm Second (Creo Parametric Default)		in	lbm	in lbm / sec^2	sec	F

Feature List

No	ID	Name	Type	Actions		Sup Order	Status
1	1	RIGHT	DATUM PLANE			---	Regenerated
2	3	TOP	DATUM PLANE			---	Regenerated
3	5	FRONT	DATUM PLANE			---	Regenerated
4	7	PRT_CSYS_DEF	COORDINATE SYSTEM			---	Regenerated
5	39	---	PROTRUSION			---	Regenerated
6	74	---	PROTRUSION			---	Regenerated
7	114	---	HOLE			---	Regenerated

Figure 16–10

The following icons in the *Tools* tab can be used to investigate parent/child relationships in the model.

- (Feature)

- (Reference Viewer)

- $d=$ (Relations and Parameters)

Feature

The **Feature** option displays all of the information on a selected feature. Figure 16–11 shows all of the information for feature number 7. All parents of the selected feature are listed in the *Parents* area in the Creo Parametric Browser.

*The **Feature List** and **Model** options display all of the features in the model. The feature number, id, name, type, suppression order and regeneration status of each feature is reported in the Browser window.*

Figure 16–11

Reference Viewer

The Reference Viewer is available to display the parent/child relationships for selected features. To open it, select the required feature and click 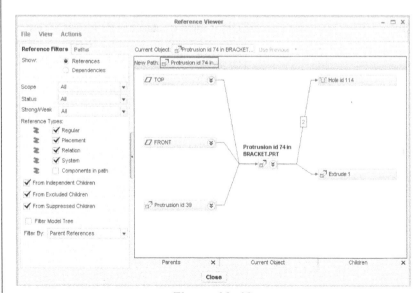 (Reference Viewer). The Reference Viewer dialog box opens as shown in Figure 16–12.

Figure 16–12

An arrow between two objects indicates a reference. When multiple references exist, a number displays on the arrow, indicating the exact number of references. Right-click on a reference arrow and select **Display Full Path** to display the full reference path between objects. The Full Path Display dialog box opens as shown in Figure 16–13.

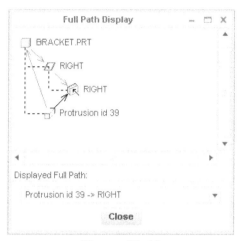

Figure 16–13

You can filter the Reference Viewer to display objects with parents only or objects with children only. To display objects with parents only, select **Parent References** in the Filter By drop-down list.

Using the Reference Viewer dialog box, you can only delete a reference when Creo Parametric identifies it as an additional reference that can be removed safely. To delete a reference, right-click on it in the Reference Viewer and select **Delete Reference**. You can use this option to delete references to rounds, chamfers, copied geometry, published geometry, annotation features, and thru-point datum curves.

Relations and Parameters

The **Relations and Parameters** option, in the Model Intent group, lists all of the relations and parameters in the part as shown in Figure 16–14.

You can also select **Relations and Parameters** *in the Model Intent group in the Model tab.*

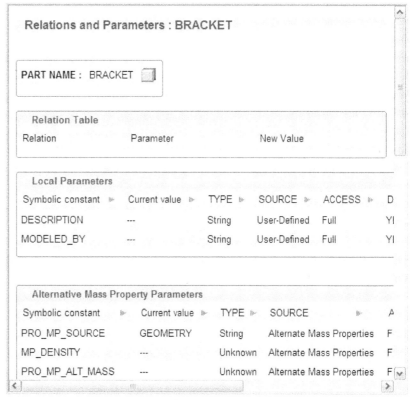

Figure 16–14

Model Player

(Model Player) in the Investigate group in the *Tools* tab, reviews the construction history of a model, one feature at a time. This option is especially helpful when working with models created by other users. The model player can give you an idea of the modeler's design intent and modeling techniques by replaying and reviewing the design.

The model player is shown in Figure 16–15. Use the control icons at the top of the dialog box to play, forward, and rewind the model. You can also specify a feature number from which to start playing the model by entering a number in the *Feat #* field. At any time while playing the model, you can click **Feat Info** and **Show Dims** to get additional information on the current feature.

Figure 16–15

The **Regenerate features** option enables you set the model player so that playing the model sequence forces the model to be regenerated instead of just displaying the current feature. The **Display each feature** option repaints the screen after each feature is displayed. You can use both of these options as required to reduce the replay time for the model, depending on your requirements.

16.4 Changing Parent/Child Relationships

 Change an existing parent/child relationship in a model using the editing tools.

The design intent of the model might change or unwanted relationships might occur as a result of modifying or deleting a parent feature. If the parent feature is modified, the child feature(s) updates with the changes. For example, if a child is dimensioned to an edge of the parent feature and modifying the parent moves this edge, the child feature moves accordingly. If the parent feature is deleted, Creo Parametric no longer has the necessary references to place the corresponding child feature(s). To avoid affecting the child when deleting the parent, there are methods to change the dependency.

You can change parent/child relationships using the **Edit Definition** and **Edit References** options by right-clicking and selecting an option in the contextual menu.

Edit Definition

The **Edit Definition** option provides you with access to the tab that was used when the feature was created. By defining new references or elements in this dialog box, you can change parent/child relationships.

You can access the **Edit Definition** option by selecting the feature in the model or in the model tree, or by right-clicking and selecting an option in the contextual menu.

Edit References

The **Edit References** option can also be used to change parent/child relationships. This option enables you to reroute the existing references to a new reference without displaying the tab that was used to create the feature.

When a feature is being rerouted, the system prompts: *Do you want to roll back the model?* The prompt indicates whether the system should display the part, as it was when the feature was created. Rolling back the model makes it easier to display the highlighted references and select appropriate alternative references.

The system highlights and toggles through each entity that was used as a reference when the feature was created. As each referenced entity is highlighted, you can select whether to maintain the reference or select an alternative reference.

Exercise 16a	Change Parent/Child Relationships I

 Recognize the possible relationships between features in the model using the Model Player.

 Discover parent/child relationships between features using the Reference Viewer.

 Change an existing parent/child relationship in a model using the editing tools.

In this exercise, you will open the model shown on the left in Figure 16–16 and you will delete the hole and chamfer so that the model displays as shown on the right. To delete these features, you have to edit their definition and establish new references within sketched features.

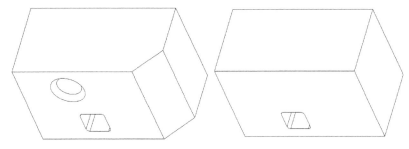

Figure 16–16

Goal

After you complete this exercise, you will be able to:

✓ **Change the references used to create features**

Task 1 - Open a part file.

1. Set the working directory to the *exercise 16a* folder.

2. Open **pc01.prt**.

Task 2 - Investigate the part.

1. Select the *Tools* tab and click  (Model Player).

2. Click ⏮ to move to the beginning of the model's feature list.

   Click ◀ to continue until the part is completely regenerated.

3. In the Model Player dialog box, click Finish .

4. Select the square cut (**Cut id 130**), right-click, and select **Edit** to display the dimensioning scheme used. The cut is located with respect to the chamfer and the hole.

5. Modify the chamfer dimension to [0.5]. What happens to the square cut? Why is it generally not a good idea to dimension to edges created by features, such as rounds and chamfers?

Task 3 - Redefine the location of the cut.

1. Select the cut, right-click, and select **Edit Definition**. Right-click and select **Edit Internal Sketch** to activate the *Sketch* tab. Redimension the cut to the right side surface of the base feature, not the chamfer edge.

*You can access the sketch tab by right-clicking and selecting **Edit Internal Sketch**.*

2. Complete the sketch and definition of the feature.

3. Delete the chamfer. Is the square cut affected?

Task 4 - Delete the hole.

1. Select the hole, right-click, and select **Delete**. The Delete dialog box opens indicating that the hole has children, as shown in Figure 16–17. To delete the hole, you must fix the references for the children.

Figure 16–17

2. Click [Cancel] to close the Delete dialog box and cancel the **Delete** action.

3. Select the hole, right-click, and select **Info > Reference Viewer**. The Reference Information Window opens as shown in Figure 16–18, indicating that the cut and chamfer are children.

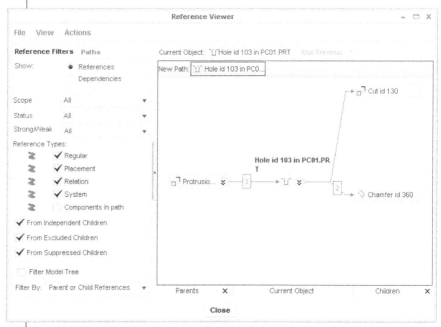

Figure 16–18

4. Right-click on the Cut in the Reference Viewer window and select **Display Full Path**. This displays the references used as shown in Figure 16–19. The hole axis A_2 was used as a reference for the cut. This must be replaced.

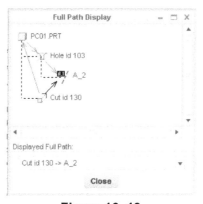

Figure 16–19

5. Close the Reference Viewer.

6. Select the cut, right-click, and select **Edit Definition**.

7. Right-click and select **Edit Internal Sketch** to activate the *Sketch* tab to edit the sketch.

8. Click ⊡ to open the References dialog box.

9. In the list of references, select **A_2(AXIS):F7(HOLE)** and delete it.

10. Select **Datum Plane TOP** as a new reference and close the References dialog box.

11. Change the resulting dimension to be strong.

12. Complete the sketch and definition of the feature.

13. Select the hole, right-click, and select **Delete**. The Delete dialog box opens again indicating that the hole has children.

14. The chamfer cannot exist without the hole, click [OK] to delete this feature as well.

15. Save the part and erase it from memory.

Exercise 16b | Tooling Jig

 Discover parent/child relationships between features using the Reference Viewer.

 Change an existing parent/child relationship in a model using the editing tools.

In this exercise, you will incorporate three design changes. You will investigate the features that require changes to see if children will be affected.

Goal

After you complete this exercise, you will be able to:

✓ **Change parent/child relationships**

Task 1 - Open a part file.

1. Set the working directory to the *exercise 16b* folder.

2. Open **tooling_jig.prt.** The model displays as shown in Figure 16–20.

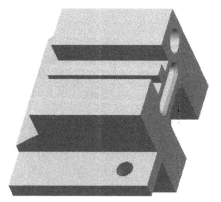

Figure 16–20

Task 2 - Investigate features of the part.

In this task, you are required to delete the CUT_AWAY feature due to a design change. Before deleting or incorporating any design change, you should always investigate the part and its features.

1. Display the part and the model tree. Select the **CUT_AWAY** feature to highlight its geometry as shown in Figure 16–21.

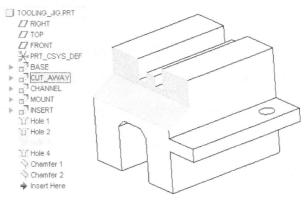

Figure 16–21

2. Verify whether the CUT_AWAY feature has any children before deleting it using the Reference Viewer. The CUT_AWAY feature does have a child (the CHANNEL feature), as shown in Figure 16–22.

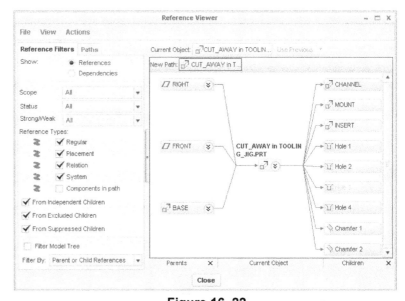

Figure 16–22

3. In the Reference Viewer, expand the CUT_AWAY feature to display the reference, as shown in Figure 16–23.

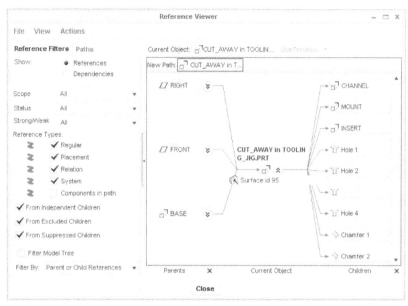

Figure 16–23

4. Select the surface reference to highlight it on the part as shown in Figure 16–24.

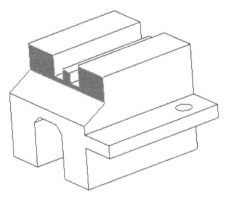

Figure 16–24

5. Close the Reference Viewer.

6. Edit the definition of the child, CHANNEL, to break its relationship with the CUT_AWAY feature. As shown in Figure 16–25, the **Through Until** depth option resulted in the parent/child relationship.

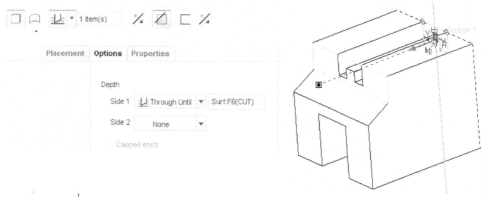

Figure 16–25

7. Change the depth option to **Through All** and complete the definition of the feature.

8. Delete the CUT_AWAY feature. The part displays as shown in Figure 16–26.

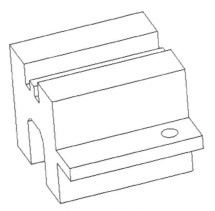

Figure 16–26

Task 3 - Change the design of the part.

Design Considerations

Due to design changes, the part must be changed to display as shown in Figure 16–27. You will not delete and recreate the features. Rather, you will edit the definition of the features, thereby changing the relationships they have with each other.

The MOUNT geometry must be moved to the other side of the part and the Hole must be moved to the top of the part

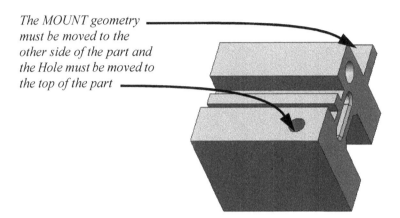

Figure 16–27

1. Edit the definition of the Hole 1 feature. Its placement references display as shown in Figure 16–28.

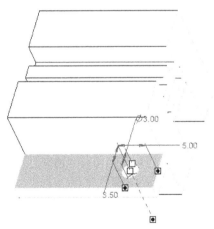

Figure 16–28

2. Change the Placement reference, as shown in Figure 16–29.

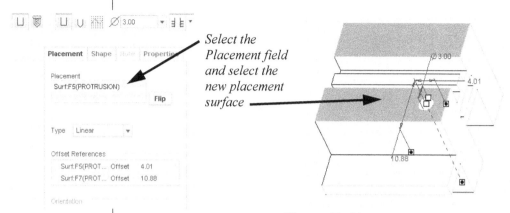

Select the Placement field and select the new placement surface

Figure 16–29

3. Select new Offset References, as shown in Figure 16–30, and edit the dimensions to the original values of [5] and [3.5].

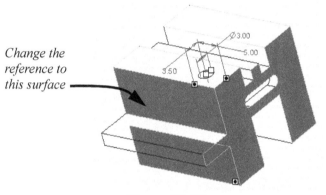

Change the reference to this surface

Figure 16–30

4. Complete the hole feature. The part displays as shown in Figure 16–31.

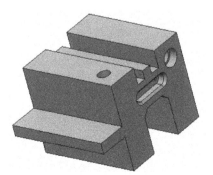

Figure 16–31

Task 4 - Change the location of a sketched feature.

1. Edit the definition of the MOUNT feature and access the *Sketch* tab. The sketch displays as shown in Figure 16–32.

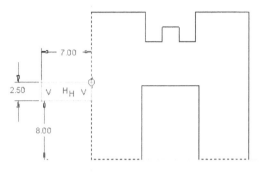

Figure 16–32

2. Click  and delete the Surf:F5(PROTRUSION) reference shown in Figure 16–33.

Figure 16–33

3. Add a reference on the opposite side of the part, as shown in Figure 16–34.

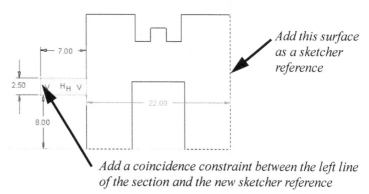

Add this surface as a sketcher reference

Add a coincidence constraint between the left line of the section and the new sketcher reference

Figure 16–34

4. Add a coincidence constraint between the left side of the section and the new sketcher reference. The sketch updates to display as shown in Figure 16–35.

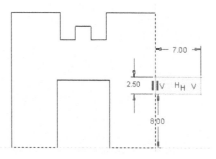

Figure 16–35

5. Complete the feature. The part displays as shown in Figure 16–36.

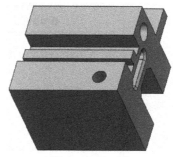

Figure 16–36

6. Save the part and erase it from memory.

Exercise 16c | (Optional) Reroute

 Discover parent/child relationships between features using the appropriate tools.

 Change an existing parent/child relationship in a model using the editing tools.

In this exercise, you will open the model shown in Figure 16–37 and make changes to the model to reflect a design change. The cut, when originally created, was sketched on a surface of the center protrusion. The design has changed so that the center protrusion is not required.

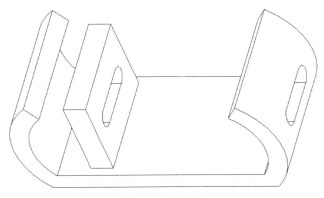

Figure 16–37

Goal

After you complete this exercise, you will be able to:

✓ **Reroute children of deleted features**

Task 1 - Reroute the cut so that the center protrusion can be deleted.

---

1. Open **pc02.prt**.

2. Change the cut so the middle protrusion can be deleted without affecting the cut as shown in Figure 16–38. Do not delete and recreate the cut.

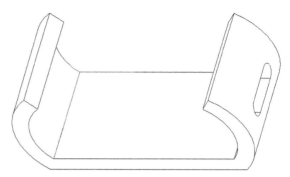

Figure 16–38

3. Save the part and erase it from memory.

Review Questions

1. A parent/child relationship is established when any solid feature is created in the model.

   a. True

   b. False

2. One pick and place feature can be a parent of another.

   a. True

   b. False

3. Which of the following actions creates a parent/child relationship when sketching a feature? (Select all that apply.)

   a. Selecting the sketching plane.

   b. Selecting the orientation plane.

   c. Maintaining the default orientation plane.

   d. Selecting sketching references.

   e. Creating an offset entity.

   f. Projecting an existing edge to create a new entity.

   g. Dimensioning the length of a line.

   h. Aligning a new entity with an existing entity.

   i. Extruding to a Blind depth.

   j. Extruding through all surfaces.

   k. Extruding to Intersect with a selected surface or plane.

4. Which of the following options can be used to investigate parent/child relationships? (Select all that apply.)

   a. Feature List

   b. Edit References

   c. Reference Viewer

   d. Model Player

5. If a parent feature must be deleted, which of the following options can be used to change the references to the child feature? (Select all that apply.)

   a. Edit

   b. Edit Definition

   c. Edit References

   d. Insert Mode

6. Which one of the following options opens the Reference Information Window dialog box shown in Figure 16–39?

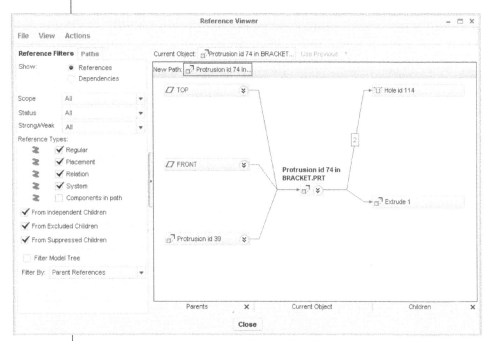

Figure 16–39

   a. *Tools* tab > **Model Player**.

   b. Right-click and select **Info > Feature List**.

   c. Right-click and select **Edit Definition**.

   d. Right-click and select **Info > Reference Viewer**.

7. Which of the following statements are true regarding the model tree shown in Figure 16–40?

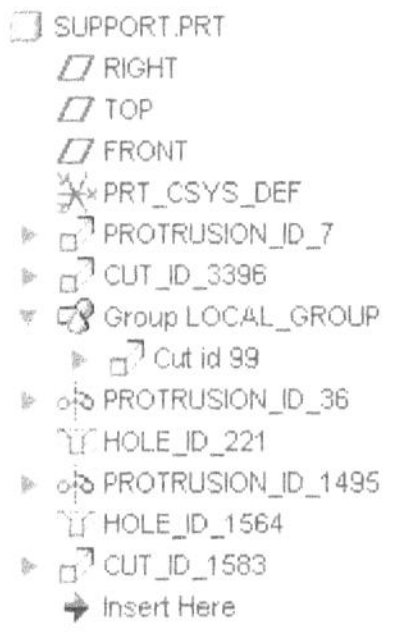

    SUPPORT.PRT
       RIGHT
       TOP
       FRONT
       PRT_CSYS_DEF
       PROTRUSION_ID_7
       CUT_ID_3396
       Group LOCAL_GROUP
          Cut id 99
       PROTRUSION_ID_36
       HOLE_ID_221
       PROTRUSION_ID_1495
       HOLE_ID_1564
       CUT_ID_1583
       Insert Here

Figure 16–40

  a. There are 2 cut features in the model.

  b. CUT_ID_1583 is a parent to PROTRUSION_ID_1495.

  c. PROTRUSION_ID_7 is the base feature of the model.

  d. HOLE_ID_221 is a parent to PROTRUSION_ID_36.

8. The Delete dialog box opens if you select and delete the hole shown in the Figure 16–41.

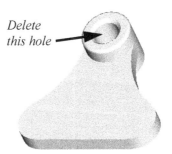

Delete this hole

Figure 16–41

  a. True

  b. False

9. What causes the Delete dialog box to open when you delete a feature?

  a. Parent/child relationships

  b. Feature Failure

  c. Feature is suppressed

  d. Feature is incomplete

10. Investigate the Reference Information Window dialog box shown in Figure 16–42. Which features are children of the current feature? (Select all that apply.)

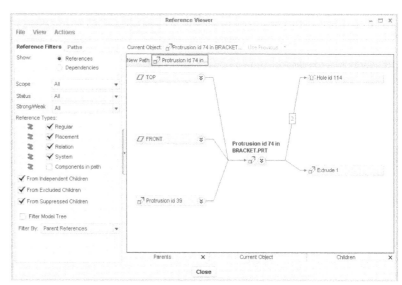

Figure 16–42

a. Hole id 114

b. Extrude 1

c. FRONT

d. Protrusion id 39

Command Summary

Button	Command	Location
	Feature	• **Ribbon:** *Tools* tab in the *Investigate* group
	Reference Viewer	• **Ribbon:** *Tools* tab in the *Investigate* group
$d=$	Relations	• **Ribbon:** *Tools* tab in the *Model Intent* group • **Ribbon:** *Model* tab in the Model Intent flyout group
	Model Player	• **Ribbon:** *Tools* tab in the *Investigate* group

Chapter 17

Feature Failure Resolution

As discussed in previous chapters, features can fail during feature creation. The failures can be resolved while you remain in the feature creation tab. This is because the failure is due to the options or elements selected while creating the feature. Regeneration failures can also occur in the model when changes are made. The resolution for regeneration failures might not be as obvious as for feature creation failures. The chapter discusses investigating and fixing failed geometry.

This chapter introduces:

      ✓**Feature Failure Overview**

      ✓**No Resolve Mode**

      ✓**Resolve Environment**

      ✓**Case Studies**

Learning Objectives

This chapter provides instruction to enable you to do the following:

17.1 Feature Failure Overview

 Identify when most failures occur and learn the two methods to correct a feature failure.

17.2 No Resolve Mode

 Diagnose and correct failures that occur using the appropriate tools.

17.3 Resolve Environment

 Diagnose and correct failures that occur using the Resolve Environment tools.

17.4 Case Studies

 Diagnose and learn how to correct common failures that occur using the appropriate tools.

17.1 Feature Failure Overview

 Identify when most failures occur and learn the two methods to correct a feature failure.

A feature failure can occur while a feature is being created, or while an existing feature is being modified or redefined.

Failures can occur for a variety of reasons. Two common examples of failed features are:

- Geometry cannot be created due to invalid or missing references.
- Dimensional changes result in geometry that cannot be calculated.

Using the No Resolve mode, you can continue working with your model even though there might be failed geometry. In this situation there are limitations to the new geometry that you can create. In addition, it is possible to save a model with failed geometry. There are two methods for fixing failed features in Creo Parametric.

Method 1

Use No Resolve Mode to modify the failed geometry as shown in Figure 17–1.

Figure 17–1

Method 2

Modify failed geometry using the Resolve Environment as shown in Figure 17–2.

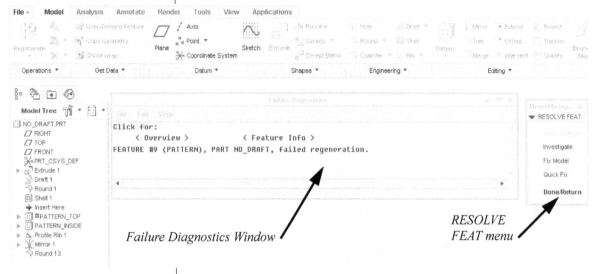

Figure 17–2

17.2 No Resolve Mode

 Diagnose and correct failures that occur using the appropriate tools.

Creo Parametric's method of handling feature regeneration failures has changed since Wildfire 5.0. When a failure is encountered during regeneration, the model continues to regenerate without going into Resolve mode.

When a failure occurs during regeneration, a warning message opens at the top of the graphics window. In addition, the model tree highlights all of the failed features and impacted child features as shown in Figure 17–3.

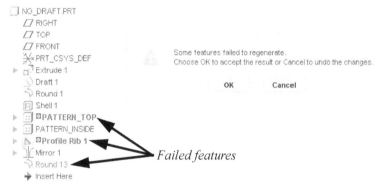

Figure 17–3

Click ⬚ **OK** to continue modeling without correcting the failed features. You can fix the problems at a later time. It is also possible to save a model with failed features.

It should be noted that in No Resolve mode, some of the operations in the Editing group cannot be used on failed features: **Mirror**, **Copy**, **Paste**, **Paste special**, and **Copy**. You cannot use the **Group** and **Pattern** operations on Failed Features. The functions of Family Tables, Inheritance Features, and Simplified Representations are affected by the regeneration failures in No Resolve mode.

Resolving Failures that Occur on Completion of a Feature

When a failure occurs on completion of a feature, the Troubleshooter dialog box might open. The display of the Troubleshooter dialog box depends on the current error. The Troubleshooter provides information on why a feature has failed as shown in Figure 17–4.

*The Troubleshooter can also be accessed by right-clicking in any collector field that contains a red or yellow dot, and selecting **What's Wrong**.*

Figure 17–4

The items listed under the feature provide you with notes to help you determine why the feature could not be created. Select each item one at a time to review the information in the lower frame of the window. Items with yellow dots indicate warnings and items with red dots indicate errors. In general, warnings provide solutions and errors explain why the current combination of references and values has failed.

After diagnosing the problem, click Close to return to the tab.

Resolving Failures that Occur on Regeneration

During regeneration, each feature in the model is recalculated. When a feature fails during regeneration, the Regeneration Manager can be opened by clicking 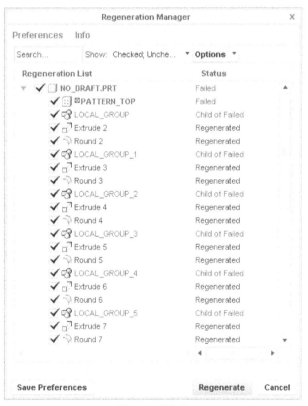 at the bottom of the window. The dialog box opens as shown in Figure 17–5.

The Regeneration Manager displays the status of the features. You can use it to perform the following actions:

- Search for features in the list.
- Apply Tree Filters to show or hide the selected items, cleared items, or both in the Regeneration List.
- Set options similar to those in the model tree
- Save the Regeneration List as a text file.
- Include or exclude features from the Regeneration List.
- Save the preference modifications.
- Change the failure handling to **Resolve Mode** vs. **No Resolve Mode**.

Figure 17–5

The Regeneration Manger also enables you to investigate the Reference Viewer. To open the Reference Viewer for a specific feature, right-click on the feature in the Regeneration Manager and select **Reference Viewer** as shown in Figure 17–6. Once in the Reference Viewer you can investigate and delete unwanted references.

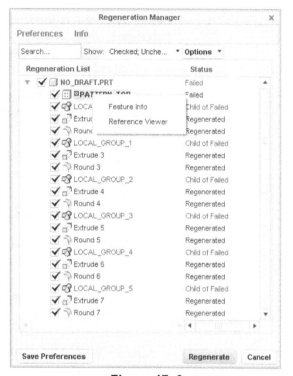

Figure 17–6

Once you have determined which modifications are required to fix the failed feature(s), use Creo Parametric's standard feature editing tools, such as **Edit Definition**, **Edit References**, and **Edit** to fix them.

- **Edit Definition:** Enables you to work on the failed feature using the tab.
- **Edit References:** Enables you to work on the failed feature by changing references.
- **Edit:** Enables you to change dimensions for any feature in the model.

17.3 Resolve Environment

 Diagnose and correct failures that occur using the Resolve Environment tools.

Before Wildfire 5.0, the Resolve Environment was used to fix failed features. By default, this environment does not display when a feature fails. However, it is possible to adjust a configuration setting so that the Resolve Environment is used when features fail.

If you want to use the Resolve Environment during feature failure as was done in earlier versions of Creo Parametric, set the regen_failure_handling configuration option to **Resolve_mode**.

Note that when using the Resolve Environment to fix a failed feature, you must resolve the failure before continuing.

Use the following general steps to resolve failures.

1. Access the resolve environment, if needed.

2. Investigate the failure.

3. Undo the previous changes made to the model, as needed.

4. Use the **Quick Fix** options to resolve the failure, as needed.

5. Use the **Fix Model** options to resolve the failure, as needed.

6. Confirm the failure resolution.

Step 1 - Access the resolve environment, if needed.

When a feature fails due to regeneration, the Failure Diagnostics window and the **RESOLVE FEAT** menu open immediately, as shown in Figure 17–7. The failure must be resolved before you can continue working on the model.

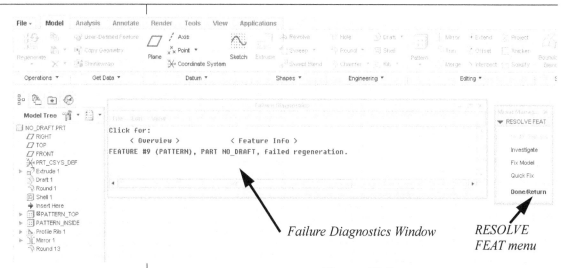

Failure Diagnostics Window   *RESOLVE FEAT menu*

Figure 17–7

Once a model has failed and the Resolve Environment is available, many options in the *File* tab are no longer available, as shown in Figure 17–8. For example, a model cannot be saved while a feature is in failure resolution.

Figure 17–8

The failed feature and all subsequent features are not regenerated or displayed in the main graphics window. For example, the **Insert Here** arrow in the model tree is placed directly before the failed feature, Profile Rib 1, as shown in Figure 17–9. Only the features before the **Insert Here** arrow are regenerated.

Figure 17–9

Step 2 - Investigate the failure.

The failed feature might be the one that was modified or it might be a feature that references it. Changes to parent features can affect child features. To investigate the failed feature, you can use options in both the Failure Diagnostics window and the **RESOLVE FEAT** menu.

Failure Diagnostics Window

The Failure Diagnostics window identifies the feature that has failed regeneration. It is identified by its feature number and type. A short description of why it has failed is displayed at the bottom of the window, as shown in Figure 17–10.

Feature # and type for the failed feature   *Description of failure*

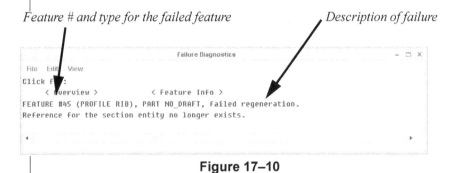

Figure 17–10

In addition to the description of the feature you can select the **<Overview>** or **<Feature Info>** options in the Failure Diagnostics window to retrieve additional information about the feature. The **<Overview>** option provides a brief description of the Resolve environment and its available options. The **<Feature Info>** option opens an html browser within Creo Parametric and enables you to review the details of the failed feature, as shown in Figure 17–11.

The commands at the top of the browser are similar to the options available in any standard HTML browser.

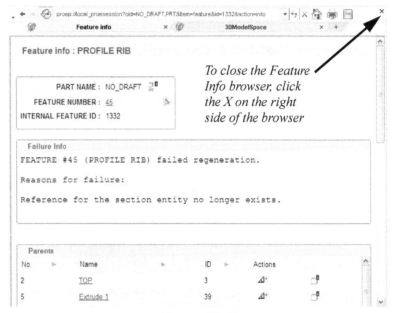

To close the Feature Info browser, click the X on the right side of the browser

Figure 17–11

RESOLVE FEAT Menu

*The **Diagnostics** option in the **INVESTIGATE** menu enables you to toggle the display of the Failure Diagnostics window on or off.*

The **Investigate** option in the **RESOLVE FEAT** menu shown in Figure 17–12, enables you to use options that can help you investigate the failed feature.

Figure 17–12

The options available in the **INVESTIGATE** menu to resolve failures are described in Table 17–1.

Table 17–1

Option	Description
List Changes	Lists the changes made to the model that caused the failure.
Show Ref	Shows the features that are referenced to the failed feature.
Failed Geom	Shows the failed geometry by highlighting it on the model.
Roll Model	Rolls the model back to one of its features to help review the failure.

Step 3 - Undo the previous changes made to the model, as needed.

Once you have investigated the reason for the failure, you need to resolve it. The **Undo Changes** option in the **RESOLVE FEAT** menu shown in Figure 17–13, provides you with a basic method for resolving the failure.

Figure 17–13

This option undoes all changes made before the regeneration that caused the failure. Using this option undoes all of the changes, even those that did not cause the failure. Once selected, you must confirm the action. The model is then automatically regenerated and returned to its pre-failure state.

Step 4 - Use the Quick Fix options to resolve the failure, as needed.

In many cases, the change that is made to the model is required and although using the **Undo Changes** option enables you to return to modeling, it does not resolve the underlying problem with the model. The **Quick Fix** option shown Figure 17–14, enables you to access several standard options that can be used to fix the failed feature.

Figure 17–14

Some of the standard options that can be accessed using Quick Fix include the following:

- **Redefine**
- **Reroute**
- **Delete**

*The **Redefine** and **Reroute** options are equivalent to the **Edit Definition** and **Edit References** options, respectively.*

Step 5 - Use the Fix Model options to resolve the failure, as needed.

The **Quick Fix** option only enables you to work on the failed feature. To make changes to any feature before the failed one you must use the **Fix Model** option in the **RESOLVE FEAT** menu, as shown in Figure 17–15.

*The **Fix Model** option is helpful when you must make changes to several features to fix the failure.*

Figure 17–15

*The **Modify** option is equivalent to the **Edit** option.*

This option opens the **FIX MODEL** menu. The options in this menu enable you to work on any feature that exists before the feature failure. The two options include the following:

- **Feature** (open the standard **FEAT** menu)
- **Modify**

Note that when using **Fix Model** with **Current Modl**, **Quick Fix** can still be used, but **Undo Changes** is no longer available. If **Fix Model** is used with **Backup Modl**, both **Quick Fix** and **Undo Changes** are available.

Step 6 - Confirm the failure resolution.

Once the failure has been resolved, the **YES/NO** menu opens enabling you to exit the Resolve environment. Once this menu opens, you can save the model before exiting the Resolve environment and select the **No** option to investigate other solutions to the feature failure.

17.4 Case Studies

 Diagnose and learn how to correct common failures that occur using the appropriate tools.

In the model shown on the left in Figure 17–16, the top linear edge of the model must be changed to an arc. The required geometry is shown on the right. To make the change, the original tab used to create the feature is displayed using the **Edit Definition** option. Once in Sketcher mode, the linear entity is deleted and an arc is sketched. Answer the following questions:

- Is the base protrusion going to fail on regeneration?
- Are any other features going to fail on regeneration? If so, why?

*The **Replace** option enables you to replace one entity with another so that all references to the original entity are automatically rerouted to the new entity.*

The design intent requires that the linear edge be changed to an arc

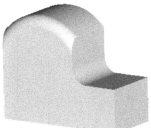

Figure 17–16

In the model shown on the left in Figure 17–17, the square cut is created by dimensioning it to a T-shaped cut. A design change is required so that the sketch of the T-shaped cut displays, as shown on the right. Answer the following questions:

- Is the base protrusion going to fail on regeneration?
- Are any other features going to fail on regeneration? If so, why?

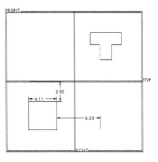 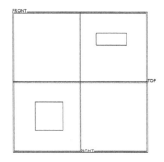

Figure 17–17

Exercise 17a | Resolve Failure

 Diagnose and correct the failures that occur using the appropriate tools.

In this exercise, you will open an existing part file that requires a design change. The part is an injection molded part that originally did not require draft due to its small size. The manufacturer has requested that 0.5 degrees of draft be added to the four outside faces. You will incorporate this change.

Goal

After you complete this exercise, you will be able to:

✓ **Resolve failures using Edit Definition**

Task 1 - Open a part file.

1. Set the working directory to the *exercise 17a* folder.

2. Open **no_draft.prt**. The model displays as shown Figure 17–18.

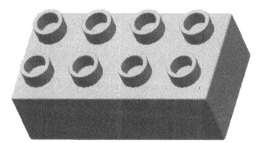

Figure 17–18

Task 2 - Activate Insert mode.

In this task you will activate Insert mode to insert a draft feature after the base feature because the draft should be created early in the feature list.

1. Drag ➜ Insert Here up and place it after Extrude 1, as shown in Figure 17–19.

NO_DRAFT.PRT
   RIGHT
   TOP
   FRONT
   PRT_CSYS_DEF
▶ Extrude 1
   Insert Here
   Round 1
   Shell 1
▶ PATTERN_TOP
▶ PATTERN_INSIDE
▶ Profile Rib 1
▶ Mirror 1
   Round 13

Figure 17–19

Task 3 - Add draft to the part.

---

1. Create a draft feature and select the four outside surfaces shown in Figure 17–20 as the surfaces to which to add the draft.

Figure 17–20

2. Select the top surface as the draft hinge, as shown in Figure 17–21. Enter [0.5] as the degree of draft (you might need to flip the draft angle direction so that the bottom of the part is larger than the top).

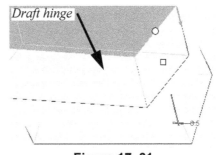

Draft hinge

Figure 17–21

3. Complete the draft feature.

Task 4 - Cancel Insert mode.

1. Drag  down to the bottom of the feature list in the model tree to cancel Insert mode. A failure occurs. In the model tree, PATTERN_TOP, Profile Rib 1, and Round 13 display in red, indicating that there has been a failure as shown in Figure 17–22.

Figure 17–22

2. In the model tree, select **PATTERN_TOP**, right click and select **Edit Definition** to redefine the pattern. The *Pattern* tab opens. Note that the pattern is a Directional pattern. The two planes that were used to define the directions are missing (indicated by the yellow dot next to 1 Plane in the *Reference* fields, as shown in Figure 17–23).

Figure 17–23

3. Select datum plane **RIGHT** as the directional reference for the 1st direction and datum plane **FRONT** as the directional reference for the 2nd direction. The pattern preview displays as shown in Figure 17–24.

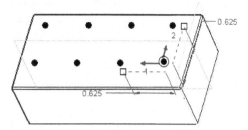

Figure 17–24

4. Complete the pattern.

Task 5 - Fix a failed feature.

1. Once the pattern has regenerated successfully, Profile Rib 1 fails.

   Click  (Regeneration Manager) at the bottom of the window. The dialog box opens as shown in Figure 17–25.

Figure 17–25

2. Right-click on Profile Rib 1 and select **Info > Reference Viewer**. The Reference Viewer shows the parent/child relationship for the Profile Rib 1.

3. Select the blue down arrows as shown in Figure 17–26. The Reference Manager indicates that there are missing references for the rib feature as shown in Figure 17–26.

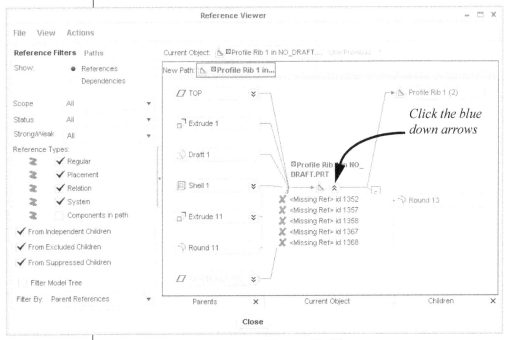

Figure 17–26

4. Click **Close** to close the Reference Viewer.

5. In the model tree, select the **Profile Rib 1** sketch, right-click and select **Edit Definition**.

6. Right-click and select **Edit Internal Sketch**. Click **Yes** to confirm the message shown in Figure 17–27.

Figure 17–27

7. Select the **MISSING REFERENCE** and click Replace to replace the missing reference as shown in Figure 17–28.

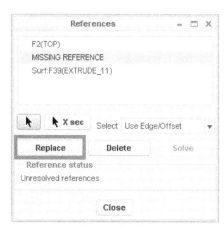

Figure 17–28

8. Select the surface shown in Figure 17–29 as the new reference.

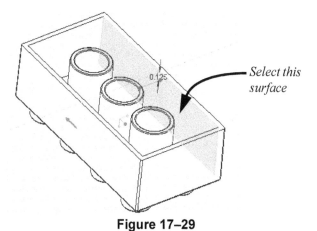

Figure 17–29

9. Click ___Solve___ in the Reference dialog box. This creates a constraint to the new reference, as shown in Figure 17–30 (there should only be one dimension in this sketch). Close the Reference dialog box.

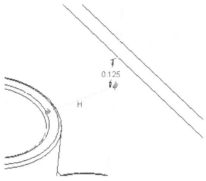

Figure 17–30

10. Complete the sketch and complete the rib feature.

11. The mirrored rib fails for the same reason. In the model tree, select the **arrow** symbol to expand Mirror 1 to display Profile Rib 1 (2).

12. Use a similar procedure to fix the second rib.

13. The completed part displays as shown in Figure 17–31.

Figure 17–31

14. Save the part and erase it from memory.

Exercise 17b | Resolving Failed Features Using the Resolve Environment

 Change the configuration option to use the resolve mode to diagnose and correct failures.

 Diagnose and correct the failures that occur using the appropriate tools.

 Avoid feature failures using the **Replace** command in the *Sketch* tab.

In this exercise, you will make several modifications to the model shown in Figure 17–32. Features that you are modifying will cause failures that must be resolved using both Quick Fix and Fix Model.

Goal

After you complete this exercise, you will be able to:

✓ **Resolve failed features using Quick Fix**
✓ **Resolve failed features using Fix Model**
✓ **Use Replace to avoid feature failures**

Task 1 - Open a part file.

---

1. Set the working directory to the *exercise 17b* folder.

2. Open **resolve.prt**. The model displays as shown in Figure 17–32.

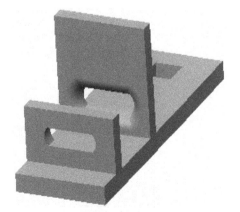

Figure 17–32

Task 2 - Turn on the Resolve Environment.

1. Select **File > Options**. Select **Configuration Editor** in the dialog box as shown in Figure 17–33.

Figure 17–33

2. Click 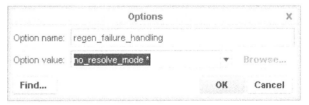 in the Creo Parametric Options dialog box to open the Options dialog box. In the *Option name* field, enter [regen_failure_handling] as shown in Figure 17–34.

Figure 17–34

3. Set the value to **resolve_mode**.

4. Make the modification and click **OK** to close the Options dialog box.

5. Click **OK** to close the Creo Parametric Options dialog box.

6. Click **No** .

Task 3 - Investigate the part.

1. Select the *Tools* tab and click (Model Player) and investigate the model features.

Task 4 - Edit a dimension of a sketch.

1. Edit CUT_1 to modify the section height, as shown in Figure 17–35. For the new value, enter [3].

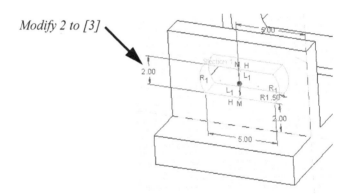

Modify 2 to [3]

Figure 17–35

The dimension does not update, and a line displays in the message window prompting you that the regeneration has failed because the dimension entered is an incompatible value, as shown in Figure 17–36.

Section regeneration failed. Incompatible dimension values.
Select a VERTEX/ENTITY/CENTER to Drag or Click on the Dimension to Modify.
● RESOLVE regeneration completed successfully.

Figure 17–36

The arcs have a radius of 1.5. This value is incompatible with the section height of 3.0. If you want to change the section height, you need to modify the arc radii at the same time.

Task 5 - Modify the sketch for an extrude.

1. In the model tree, select **Protrusion_1**. Right-click and select **Edit Definition**. Activate the *Sketch* tab by right-clicking and selecting **Edit Internal Sketch.**

2. Add a horizontal dimension of [3.00] for the top line and delete the vertical constraint on the left side of the sketch, as shown in Figure 17–37. Modify the dimensional values as shown in Figure 17–37. Do not delete any of the original entities.

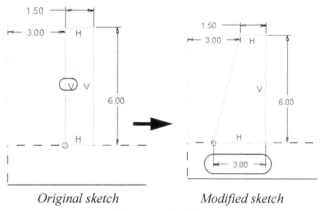

Original sketch   *Modified sketch*

Figure 17–37

3. Complete the feature redefinition.

4. The Resolve Environment opens as shown in Figure 17–38.

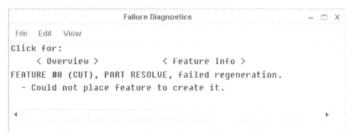

Figure 17–38

5. The CUT_1 feature fails because its sketching plane is missing. It was removed by the section modification. To resolve the failure, select **Quick Fix > Reroute > Confirm** in the Menu Manager.

6. Select datum plane **RIGHT** as an alternative sketching plane and select **Same Ref** for the remaining references.

7. Select **Yes** to exit Resolve mode. The model displays as shown in Figure 17–39.

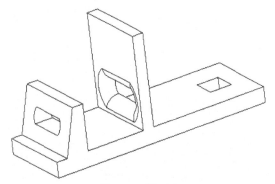

Figure 17–39

Task 6 - Modify the sketch for an extrude.

1. In the model tree, expand CUT_1. Right-click on sketch Section 1 and select **Edit Definition**.

2. Modify the feature section as shown in Figure 17–40. Delete the right arc and sketch a vertical line in its place. Select **Yes** at the prompt: *This entity is referenced by other feature(s). Continue?*

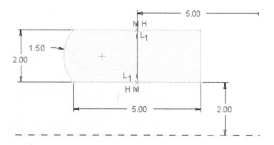

Figure 17–40

3. Complete the sketch.

4. The ROUND feature fails because one of its reference edges is missing. It was removed by the section modification. To resolve the failure, select **Quick Fix > Redefine > Confirm**.

5. Open the Sets slide-up panel and investigate the list of references. There is a red dot next to one of them. Select this reference, right-click, and select **What's wrong** as shown in Figure 17–41. The Troubleshooter window opens.

Figure 17–41

6. Read the information in the Troubleshooter window and then close the window.

7. Orient the model to the default view using <Ctrl>+<D>.

8. In the Sets slide-up panel, scroll down to the missing edge reference with a red dot in the *References* area, right-click on the failed edge reference, and select **Remove** as shown in Figure 17–42.

Figure 17–42

9. Press and hold down <Ctrl> and select the new straight edge of the cut, as shown in Figure 17–43.

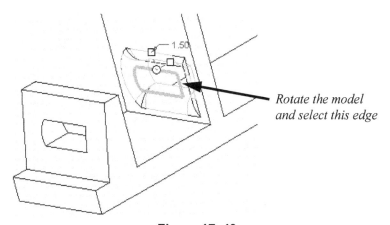

Rotate the model and select this edge

Figure 17–43

10. Complete the feature.

11. Select **Yes** to exit Resolve mode. The model displays as shown in Figure 17–44.

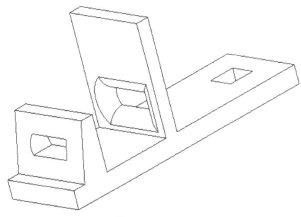

Figure 17–44

Task 7 - Modify the shape of the section for CUT_1.

---

1. In the model tree, expand Cut_1. Right-click on sketch Section 1 and select **Edit Definition**.

2. Sketch a vertical line as shown on the left in Figure 17–45. This line replaces the existing arc entity.

*You can also expand the Operations flyout panel and select **Replace**.*

3. Select the arc from the sketch, right-click, and select **Replace**.

   Select the new vertical line to be replaced. Click ^{Yes} to remove the dimension and complete the replace action. The sketch displays as shown on the right in Figure 17–45.

Replace this arc with the vertical line

Sketch this vertical line

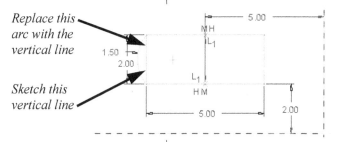

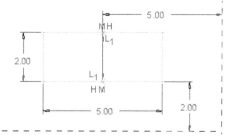

Figure 17–45

4. Complete the feature redefinition. The model displays as shown in Figure 17–46.

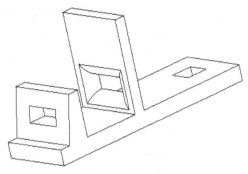

Figure 17–46

The ROUND feature has been modified without failure. This is because you replaced the old section entity with the new one.

Task 8 - Modify the shape of the section for the BASE feature.

1. Edit the definition of the BASE feature sketch.

2. Modify the sketch as shown in Figure 17–47. Sketch an arc, which will replace the existing vertical line entity. Then select **Edit >**

   Replace and follow the system instructions. Click Yes to remove the dimension and complete the replace action.

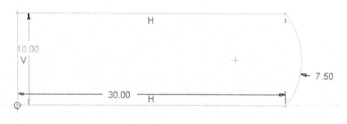

Figure 17–47

3. Complete the feature redefinition.

4. The CUT_2 feature fails because one of its dimension references is missing. It was removed by the section modification. To resolve the failure, select **Quick Fix > Redefine > Confirm**.

In the original model, the position of the section of CUT_2 is dimensioned to the right vertical planar surface of the BASE feature.

5. Redefine the feature section. Remove the failed sketcher reference and add a new one. Select the new cylindrical surface from the BASE feature as a reference. Modify the feature section as shown in Figure 17–48.

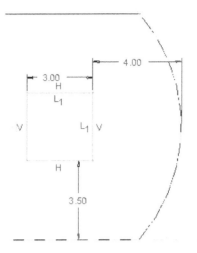

Figure 17–48

6. Complete the feature redefinition.

7. Select **Yes** to exit Resolve mode. The model displays as shown in Figure 17–49.

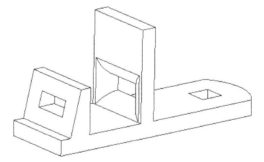

Figure 17–49

8. Save the part and erase it from memory.

9. Change the *regen_failure_handling* configuration option back to **no_resolve_mode**.

Review Questions

1. When a feature fails you can continue to model without fixing the failed feature.

   a. True

   b. False

2. When the Resolve Environment is active, which of the following options are available for use? (Select all that apply.)

   a. Undo Changes

   b. Save

   c. Investigate

   d. Edit Definition/Redefine

3. When a feature fails, the failed feature and all subsequent features are not regenerated and are not displayed in the main window.

   a. True

   b. False

4. Which one of the following options enables you to investigate why the failure occurred?

   a. Overview

   b. Feature Info

   c. Resolve Hints

   d. Investigate

5. Which one of the following options enables you to make changes to any feature that exists before the failed feature?

   a. Fix Model

   b. Quick Fix

6. Which one of the following options enables you to only make changes to the failed feature to resolve the failure?

   a. Fix Model

   b. Quick Fix

7. The **Undo Changes** option enables you to resolve the failure while at the same time maintaining the change that originally caused the failure.

   a. True

   b. False

8. Clicking **Cancel** in the message box shown in Figure 17–50, enables you to fix the failure while maintaining the change that originally caused the failure.

Some features failed to regenerate.
Choose OK to accept the result or Cancel to undo the changes.

OK   Cancel

Figure 17–50

   a. True

   b. False

9. Once a failure has been resolved and before confirming the existing resolve environment, the **Save** option becomes available. Why? (Select all that apply.)

   a. You can save the model before exiting the Resolve environment.

   b. You can select the **No** option to investigate other solutions to the feature failure.

   c. To close Creo Parametric.

   d. You can create a pattern.

Command Summary

Button	Command	Location
	Regeneration Manager	• **Ribbon:** *Model* tab in the *Operations* group

Chapter 18

Sweeps

Sweep features can be used to create advanced geometry that standard extrusions cannot create. They enable you to sketch a cross-section and sweep it along a defined trajectory.

This chapter introduces:

> ✓ **Creating a Sweep Feature**

Learning Objectives

This chapter provides instruction to enable you to do the following:

18.1 Creating a Sweep Feature

 Create a sweep feature and set the necessary options in the *Sweep* tab to create the required geometry.

18.1 Creating a Sweep Feature

 Create a sweep feature and set the necessary options in the *Sweep* tab to create the required geometry.

A sweep feature form enables you to create advanced geometry that cannot be created using an extrusion. Basic sweep features enable you to create geometry by sweeping a cross-section along a single trajectory, as shown in Figure 18–1.

Advance sweeps using multiple trajectories are explained in the Creo Parametric: Advanced Part class.

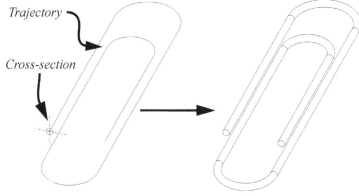

Figure 18–1

Use the following steps as a general guideline to create a sweep:

1. Start the creation of a sweep.

2. Define the trajectory for the sweep.

3. Sketch the cross-section for the sweep.

Step 1 - Start the creation of a sweep.

To start the creation of a sweep, click ✎ (Sweep) in the Shapes group in the *Model* tab. The *Sweep* tab displays as shown in Figure 18–2.

Figure 18–2

A sweep can add or remove material by clicking ⬚. You can also click ⌐ and specify a thickness value.

Step 2 - Define the trajectory for the sweep.

The trajectory defines how the geometry of the feature is created. The entities can be an open or closed loop. The trajectory can be a selected edge, curve, or sketch that exists in the model. Once you select a trajectory it displays in the Reference panel as shown in Figure 18–3. The cross-section remains normal to the trajectory as it is swept.

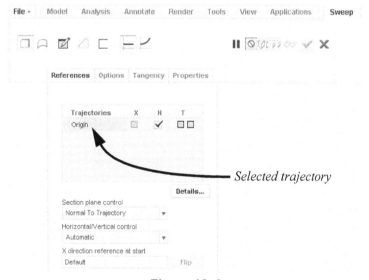

Figure 18–3

Select Trajectory

You can select existing edges or datum curves to define the trajectory for the sweep. Selecting the Reference panel and clicking **Details...** can be used to select multiple curves to define the trajectory as shown in Figure 18–4.

Figure 18–4

Sketched Trajectory

You can sketch the trajectory by clicking ⌇ (Datum) and clicking ⌇. This creates a sketched curve that is copied into the swept feature with an associated link. Any subsequent modification to the sketch is reflected in the swept feature.

• You can also select the *View* tab and click ⌇ (Sketch).

Options Panel for Sweep

If the trajectory forms an open loop and solid geometry already exists in the model, you can define whether the cross-section merges to the existing geometry at both ends of the trajectory or remains free. The option is shown in Figure 18–5.

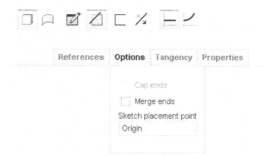

Figure 18–5

By default the merge option is not selected. This option enables the cross-section to remain perpendicular to the trajectory at all points along it. For the **Merge Ends** option, at least one end of the swept feature must have a surface to merge into. If **Merge Ends** is selected and is not a viable option, the feature aborts. The sweep shown on the right in Figure 18–6 is created using the **Merge Ends** option, while the model shown on the left is created without the option.

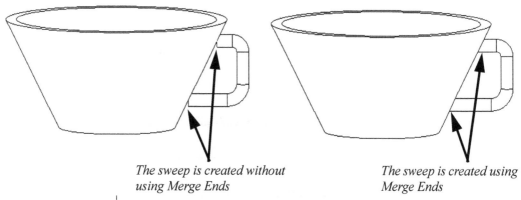

The sweep is created without using Merge Ends

The sweep is created using Merge Ends

Figure 18–6

Start Point

The start point of a trajectory defines the location where the cross-section is sketched. The start point, identified with an arrow, must be at one of the trajectory endpoints for an open trajectory. It can be at any internal point for a closed trajectory.

Once a trajectory has been selected from existing geometry, you can change the start point by selecting the References panel and clicking Details... . This opens the Chain dialog box as shown in Figure 18–7.

Select the *Options* tab and click Flip to move the start point to the other end of the trajectory. You can also change the start point by selecting the arrow on the trajectory, right-click, and select **Flip Chain Direction**.

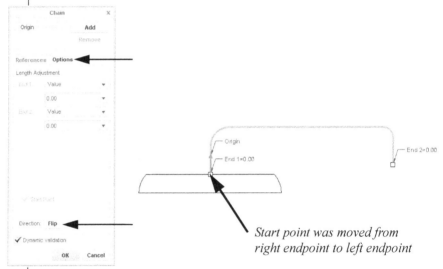

Start point was moved from right endpoint to left endpoint

Figure 18–7

Step 3 - Sketch the cross-section for the sweep.

Once the trajectory has been defined, click 🖉. The *Sketch* tab becomes active. Cross-hairs display identifying the start point on an open trajectory, as shown on the left in Figure 18–8. Sketch the cross-section for the sweep relative to the start point. It maintains this relationship along the entire trajectory.

Consider clicking 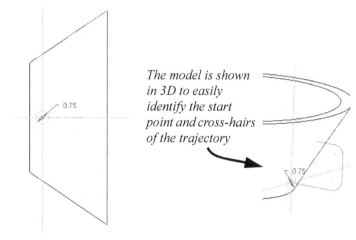 *to orient the model in 2D. This makes it easier to sketch and locate the cross-hairs in the sketch.*

The model is shown in 3D to easily identify the start point and cross-hairs of the trajectory

Figure 18–8

Figure 18–9 shows an example of a closed trajectory.

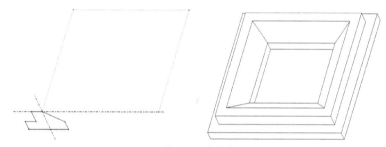

Figure 18–9

A cross-section does not have to lie directly on the cross-hairs. If the cross-section is offset it maintains the offset as it travels along the trajectory.

If the cross-section overlaps itself as it travels along the trajectory, the feature might abort, as shown in Figure 18–10. If this occurs, edit the definition of the cross-section or trajectory to correct the failure.

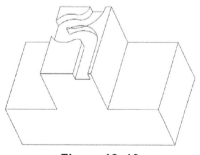

Figure 18–10

Sweeps can be made along trajectories consisting of non-tangent entities. Trajectory entities that are not tangent produce mitered corners, as shown in Figure 18–11.

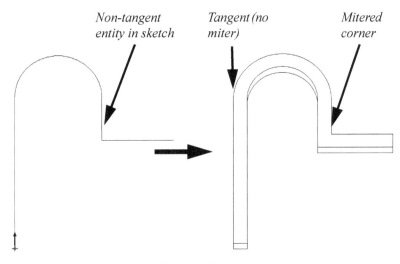

Figure 18–11

Exercise 18a | Paper Clip

 Create the sweep by selecting the curve for the trajectory.

 Sketch the profile for the swept feature by changing the start point.

 Sketch the profile entities to create required swept geometry.

In this exercise, you will create a part using a sweep as the base feature as shown in Figure 18–12. A sweep must have a trajectory and a section. A trajectory can be sketched or selected and you will select a trajectory.

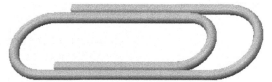

Figure 18–12

Goal

After you complete this exercise, you will be able to:

✓ **Create a swept protrusion**

Task 1 - Open a part file.

---

1. Set the working directory to the *exercise 18a* folder.

2. Open **paper_clip.prt.** The part contains a completed sketch as shown in Figure 18–13. You use this sketch as the trajectory for the sweep.

Figure 18–13

3. Click  (Sweep) in the Shapes group in the *Model* tab.

4. Select **Sketch 1** as the trajectory.

   The system automatically selects a start point as shown in Figure 18–14.

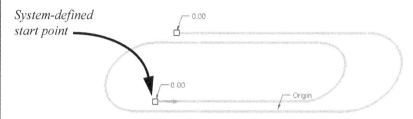

Figure 18–14

Task 2 - Change the start point for a sweep.

Design Considerations

The location of the start point is the location at which the section will be sketched. Its location is a user preference and has no real impact on feature creation.

1. To change the start point, right-click on the arrow and select **Flip Chain Direction**, as shown in Figure 18–15.

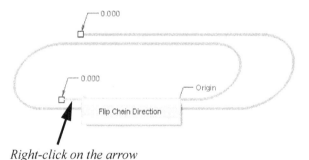

Figure 18–15

2. This changes the start point and moves it to the other end of the trajectory as shown in Figure 18–16.

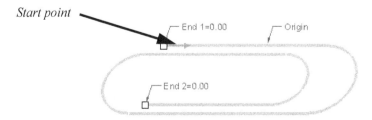

Figure 18–16

Task 3 - Sketch a section for the sweep.

1. Now that the trajectory has been defined, click 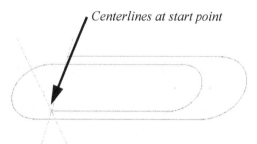 to sketch the cross section.

2. The *Sketch* tab becomes active and displays horizontal and vertical center lines at the start point, as shown in Figure 18–17.

Centerlines at start point

Figure 18–17

3. Sketch and dimension the cross-section for the paper clip, as shown in Figure 18–18.

Figure 18–18

4. Click ✓ (OK) to complete the sketch.

5. Click  to complete the feature.

6. Orient the model to the Default View. The part displays as shown in Figure 18–19.

Figure 18–19

7. Save the part and erase it from memory.

Exercise 18b | Swept Features

 Sketch appropriate path and profile entities to create required swept geometry.

 Select existing edges in the model as the path for a sweep feature.

 Set the necessary options in the *Sweep* tab and create the profile entities to create the required swept geometry.

 Edit a sweep feature and change the feature options to merge ends.

In this exercise, you will create the part shown in Figure 18–20.

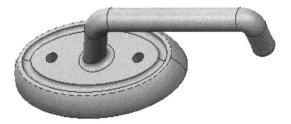

Figure 18–20

Goal | After you complete this exercise, you will be able to:

✓ **Create swept features**
✓ **Edit the definition of swept features**
✓ **Edit swept features**

Task 1 - Open a part file.

1. Set the working directory to the *exercise 18b* folder.

2. Open **door_handle.prt**. The part displays as shown in Figure 18–21.

Figure 18–21

Task 2 - Create a sketched swept protrusion.

In this task, you will create the swept protrusion for the handle, as shown in Figure 18–22.

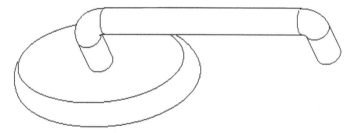

Figure 18–22

1. Click 🗡 (Sweep) in the Shapes group in the *Model* tab.

2. Expand 〰 (Datum) in the *Sweep* tab and click ⌢ to sketch a trajectory.

3. For the sketching plane for the trajectory, select datum plane **FRONT.**

4. Select datum plane **RIGHT** as the Right reference plane.

5. Click **Sketch** to activate the *Sketch* tab.

6. Sketch and dimension the trajectory, as shown in Figure 18–23.

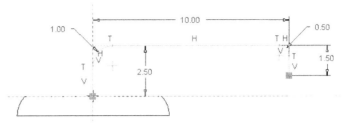

Figure 18–23

7. Click ✓ (OK) to complete the sketch for the trajectory.

8. Click ▶ to activate the *Sweep* tab. Note that the new sketch is selected as the trajectory.

9. If necessary, change the start point by right-clicking on the arrow and selecting **Flip Chain Direction**. The model displays as shown in Figure 18–24.

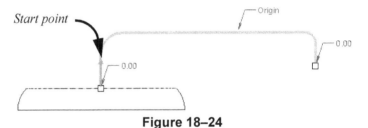

Figure 18–24

10. Click ✐ to sketch the cross-section.

11. Click ⟳ to orient the view. The crosshairs display, indicating the start point for the trajectory. Sketch and dimension the cross-section at the intersection of the crosshairs, as shown in Figure 18–25.

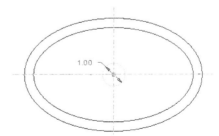

Figure 18–25

12. Click ✓ (OK) to complete the cross-section. Complete the feature.

13. Rename the sweep and the sketch you just created as [HANDLE] and [SKETCH_HANDLE], as shown in Figure 18–26.

Figure 18–26

14. Set the orientation to the Default view. The model displays as shown in Figure 18–27.

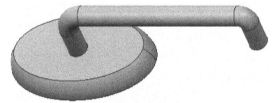

Figure 18–27

Task 3 - Create a swept cut using a selected trajectory.

1. Click ⬚ (Sweep) in the *Model* tab.

2. Click ◺ in the *Sweep* tab.

3. Select the top edge of the base protrusion for the trajectory as shown in Figure 18–28. If necessary drag the start point to the location as shown in Figure 18–28.

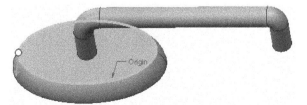

Figure 18–28

4. Click 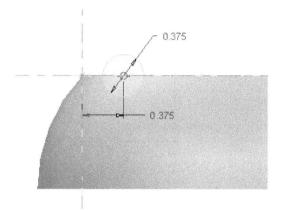 in the *Sweep* tab, to sketch the cross-section.

5. Sketch and dimension a circle section, as shown in Figure 18–29.

Figure 18–29

6. Click ✔ (OK) to complete the cross-section.

7. Click ✔ to complete the feature. The model displays as shown in Figure 18–30.

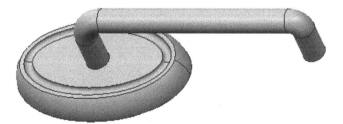

Figure 18–30

Task 4 - Edit the trajectory of the swept handle.

1. In the model tree, select **SKETCH_HANDLE**.

2. Right-click and select **Edit**.

3. The trajectory dimensions display as shown in Figure 18–31. Edit dimension 10 as [7].

You can also drag the open arrow on the sketch to change the dimension to [7]

Change this dimension to [7]

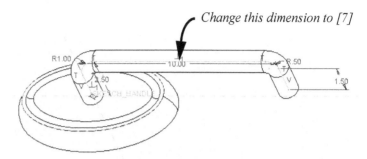

Figure 18–31

4. Regenerate the model. It displays as shown in Figure 18–32.

Figure 18–32

Task 5 - Edit the definition of the swept handle.

1. In the model tree, select **SKETCH_HANDLE**, right-click and select **Edit Definition** to change the trajectory sketch.

2. Add the angular dimension and delete the vertical constraint, as shown in Figure 18–33.

Add this angular dimension

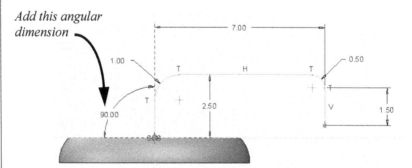

Figure 18–33

3. Edit the angular value as [110] and the horizontal dimension as [8], as shown in Figure 18–34.

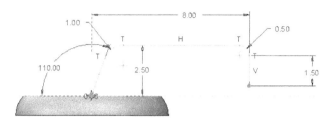

Figure 18–34

4. Complete the sketch.

5. Display the resulting geometry. Note that the handle does not extend up to the base due to the angle of trajectory, as shown in Figure 18–35.

Figure 18–35

6. Edit the definition of the HANDLE.

7. Select the Options panel and select **Merge ends**.

8. Complete the feature. The model displays as shown in Figure 18–36.

Figure 18–36

Task 6 - Create additional features on the model (optional).

1. Create two 0.5 diameter holes as shown in Figure 18–37.

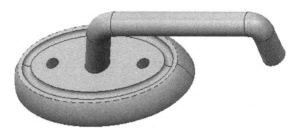

Figure 18–37

2. Create a round on the two edges as shown in Figure 18–38.

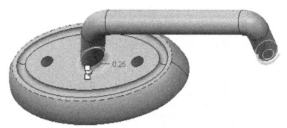

Figure 18–38

3. Save the part and erase it from memory.

Exercise 18c | Swept Base Features

 Create required swept geometry by sketching appropriate path and profile entities.

Goal

After you complete this exercise, you will be able to:

✓ **Create base features using sweeps**

Task 1 - Create new parts.

1. Set the working directory to the *exercise 18c* folder.

2. Create the parts shown in Figure 18–39 using swept protrusions.

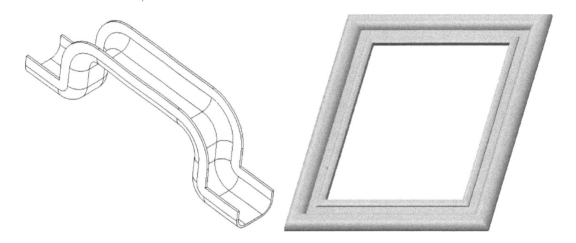

Figure 18–39

Review Questions

1. A Sweep can be used in a model to add or remove material.

    a. True

    b. False

2. Which of the following statements are true regarding Sweeps?

    a. A Sweep creates a single feature whose geometry is blended between multiple sub-sections.

    b. A Sweep creates a single feature whose geometry is swept along a defined trajectory.

    c. A Sweep can only be added to the model after the base protrusion has been created.

    d. The trajectory for a sweep must be sketched.

3. What are the two elements that must be defined to create a Sweep feature?

    a. Trajectory and section

    b. Trajectory and depth

    c. Section and depth

4. Why is it important to rename your features in the model tree?

    a. To identify the feature.

    b. To edit the feature.

    c. To organize the features in alphabetical order.

5. You can select a trajectory and a cross-section in the *Sweep* tab.

    a. True

    b. False

6. The start point of an open loop trajectory can be anywhere on the curve.

    a. True

    b. False

7. Which of the following criteria are required to use the **Merge Ends** or **Free Ends** options? (Select all that apply.)

   a. Solid geometry already exists in the model.

   b. The trajectory forms a closed loop.

   c. The trajectory forms an open loop.

   d. The cross-section is circular.

8. Which of the following are true statements regarding the start point of a trajectory? (Select all that apply.)

   a. The start point defines the location where the cross-section is sketched.

   b. Start points must be located at the start or end of an open trajectory.

   c. To change the start point for a trajectory, select the Reference panel and click `Details...` .

   d. To change the start point for a selected trajectory, right-click on the arrow and select **Flip Chain Direction**.

9. The cross-section remains perpendicular as it follows the trajectory.

   a. True

   b. False

10. The trajectory cannot contain any sharp corners.

   a. True

   b. False

Command Summary

Button	Command	Location
	Sweep	• **Ribbon:** *Model* tab in the *Shapes* group

Chapter 19

Blend Feature Forms

Blends are an additional feature form that enables you to create complex geometry. Blends enable you to sketch or select multiple cross-sections between created geometry.

This chapter introduces:

✓ **Create a Blend Feature**

Learning Objectives

This chapter provides instruction to enable you to do the following:

19.1 Create a Blend Feature

 Create a blend feature and set the necessary options in the *Blend* tab by sketching sections and ensuring they each have the same number of entities.

 Sketch or select the section for the blend feature using the tools in the *Sketch* tab.

 Ensure each section has the same number of entities to create the blend using Blend Vertex or Trim tools.

19.1 Create a Blend Feature

 Create a blend feature and set the necessary options in the *Blend* tab by sketching sections and ensuring they each have the same number of entities.

 Sketch or select the section for the blend feature using the tools in the *Sketch* tab.

 Ensure each section has the same number of entities to create the blend using Blend Vertex or Trim tools.

A blend feature enables you to create advanced geometry that cannot be created using a single extrusion. The geometry is defined by blending between multiple sub-sections, as shown in Figure 19–1.

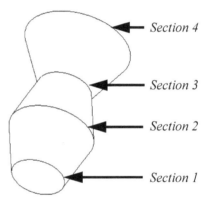

Figure 19–1

A blend can either remove or add material to a model.

Use the following general steps to create a parallel blend feature:

1. Start the creation of the blend feature.

2. Specify additional options for a blend.

3. Select or sketch the sections for the blend.

4. Complete the feature.

Step 1 - Start the creation of the blend feature.

To start the creation of a blend, select **Shapes > Blend** in the *Model* tab. The menu structure is shown in Figure 19–2.

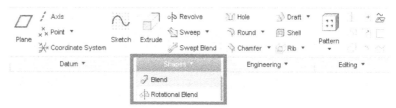

Figure 19–2

The *Blend* tab displays as shown in Figure 19–3.

Figure 19–3

Rotational and General Blends are discussed in Creo Parametric: Advanced Part Design.

This training guide discusses simple parallel blend types. They are sections that are parallel with one another.

Step 2 - Specify additional options for a blend.

A blend can be created using the **Smooth** or **Straight** option as shown in Figure 19–4.

Figure 19–4

For a Straight Blend, the vertices of each adjacent section are connected with linear edges, as shown in Figure 19–5.

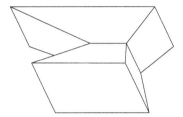

Figure 19–5

For a Smooth Parallel Blend, a spline passes through the vertices of the intermediate sections, as shown in Figure 19–6.

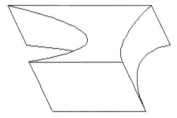

Figure 19–6

Step 3 - Select or sketch the sections for the blend.

A blend is created from a multiple sections. At least two sections are required to create a blend. Sections for the blend can be selected or sketched.

Selected Sections

To select the sections, click 〰 or select **Selected sections** in the Sections panel, as shown in Figure 19–7. Click `Insert` to select additional sections.

Figure 19–7

Sketched Section

As with any sketched feature, you must select a sketching plane and sketch orientation plane. You can select planes or surfaces as references. The sketch references must also be defined and can be datum planes, surfaces, edges, or vertices. Sketching the section for the blend is done using the *Sketch* tab and the tools that have been discussed previously.

Use the following steps to create a blend using sketched sections.

1. Click ⌐Define...⌐ in the Sections slide-up panel, as shown in Figure 19–8 or right-click and select **Define Internal Sketch**. Select a sketching plane, orientation plane, and additional references.

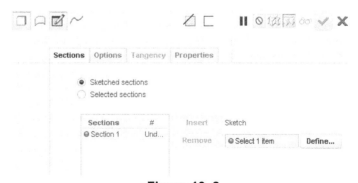

Figure 19–8

2. Sketch the first section using the *Sketch* tab and click ✔ (OK).

3. If necessary, click **Insert** to create a new section.

4. Specify a depth between the sections in the Sections panel.

You can also click ↦ or ⊥ in the Blend tab to specify the Offset dimensional or Reference options.

The depth is determined by the offset option of the next section. You can use **Offset dimensional**, as shown in Figure 19–9, and enter a specified value. You can also select **Reference** and select an existing datum plane or surface, as shown in Figure 19–10.

Figure 19–9

Figure 19–10

*You can also right-click and select **Sketch**.*

5. Click **Sketch...** in the Sections panel or ✎ in the *Blend* tab to create an additional section. At least two sections are required to create a blend.

6. Sketch the next section and click ✔ (OK).

7. Add additional sections as needed.

Vertices

Each sub-section can contain geometry of any shape. However, each sub-section must have an equal number of vertices. Consider the following techniques for accomplishing this.

Equal Entities

⌐ (Divide) can be used in conjunction with construction entities to split the entities as required. For example, a circle must be broken into four arcs to blend a circle with a square, as shown in Figure 19–11.

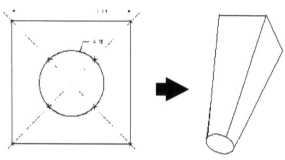

Figure 19–11

Blend Vertex

*You can also right-click and select **Blend Vertex**.*

The **Blend Vertex** option can be used if the design intent calls for unequal numbers of vertices per section. Figure 19–12 shows a square section being blended with a triangular section. A Blend Vertex is placed on a vertex of the triangle, enabling the extra vertex from the square to blend to this point. To set a vertex for blending, select the vertex, and select **Setup > Feature Tools > Blend Vertex**.

A blended vertex cannot be located at the start point of a section.

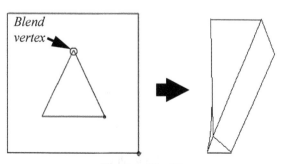

Figure 19–12

Sketcher Point

The first and last sub-sections in a parallel blend can consist of a sketcher point. This enables you to blend a sub-section with multiple entities to a single point, as shown in Figure 19–13. To add a sketcher point, click ✕ and place the point on the sketch, as needed.

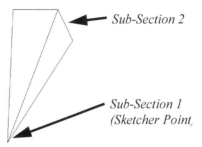

Sub-Section 2

*Sub-Section 1
(Sketcher Point,*

Figure 19–13

Start Point

A start point (indicated by a orange arrow) is located at the first vertex sketched in each sub-section. Creo Parametric creates the geometry for a blend by connecting these start points. It continues to match each subsequent vertex moving in a clockwise direction to create the feature.

To move the start point, select the vertex that is going to be the start point and select **Setup > Feature Tools > Start Point** to move the start point or right-click and select **Start Point**. Figure 19–14 shows how the blended geometry can be affected when the start points for each section are not located in the same relative location for each sub-section.

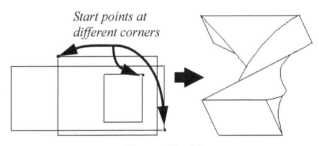

*Start points at
different corners*

Figure 19–14

Step 4 - Complete the feature.

Once all the sections and options have been specified, click to complete the feature.

Exercise 19a | Keyboard Key

 Create a blend feature by sketching two sections.

In this exercise, you will create a key used on a keyboard. You will create the base feature using a blend with two sections, finish the part with rounds, and then shell the part. The completed part is shown in Figure 19–15.

Figure 19–15

Goal

After you complete this exercise, you will be able to:

✓ **Create a two-section parallel blend**

Task 1 - Create a new part file.

1. Set the working directory to the *exercise 19a* folder.

2. Create a new part file named [key].

3. In the *Model* tab, select **Shapes > Blend**. The *Blend* tab activates as shown in Figure 19–16.

Figure 19–16

*You can also right-click and select **Define Internal Sketch**.*

4. Click **Sections** and click **Define...**. The Sketch dialog box opens.

5. Select datum plane **TOP** as the sketching plane and set datum plane **FRONT** to face bottom.

6. Click **Sketch** in the Sketch dialog box.

7. Expand □ ▾ and click ▣ (Center Rectangle). Select the center point at the intersection of datum plane **FRONT** and **RIGHT**.

8. Sketch and dimension a square as shown in Figure 19–17, ensuring that the lines are equal lengths.

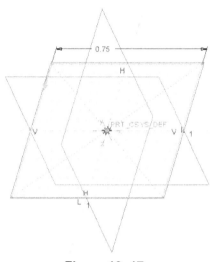

Figure 19–17

9. Click ✓ (OK) to complete the sketch.

10. Select the Section panel and enter [0.25] for the depth value, as show in Figure 19–18. You can also change the depth value using the drag handle in the view window.

Figure 19–18

*You can also click 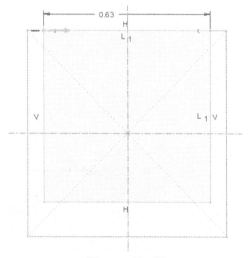 in the Blend tab or right-click and select **Sketch**.*

11. Click [Sketch...] to create the next section.

12. Sketch a second square, as shown in Figure 19–19. Begin the sketch in the upper left corner and permit coincidence with the horizontal line of the first sketch. Verify that the lines are of equal lengths. Make sure the start points of both sections are the same. If the start points do not line up, select the desired location for the start point, right-click, and select **Start Point**.

Figure 19–19

13. Click  (Ok).

14. Complete the blend feature. The completed blend displays as shown in Figure 19–20.

Figure 19–20

Task 2 - Create an extruded cut.

1. Create an extruded cut. Click 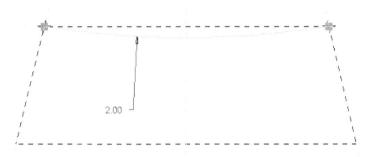 to removed material.

2. Use datum plane FRONT as the sketch plane. The system will select datum plane **RIGHT** to face Right.

3. Add the appropriate sketch references and sketch a single arc, as shown in Figure 19–21.

2.00

Figure 19–21

4. Complete the sketch.

5. Remove material on both sides of the sketch. The *Extrude* tab and model display as shown in Figure 19–22.

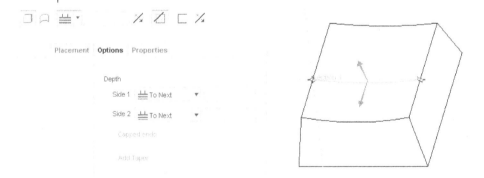

Placement **Options** Properties

Depth

Side 1 ⬌ To Next ▼

Side 2 ⬌ To Next ▼

Capped ends

Add Taper

Figure 19–22

The completed extrude displays as shown in Figure 19–23.

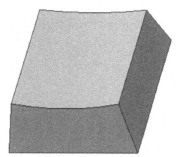

Figure 19–23

Task 3 - Create rounds.

1. Create a [0.063] radius round on the four edges shown in Figure 19–24.

Figure 19–24

2. Create a [0.01] radius round on the edge shown in Figure 19–25.

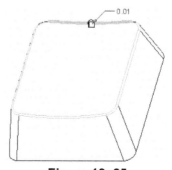

Figure 19–25

Task 4 - Shell the part.

1. Shell the part with a thickness of [0.02]. Remove the bottom surface, as shown in Figure 19–26.

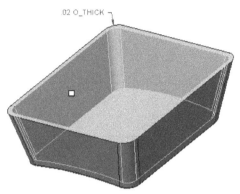

Figure 19–26

2. Set the orientation to the Default view. The model displays as shown in Figure 19–27.

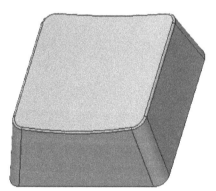

Figure 19–27

3. Save the part and erase it from memory.

Exercise 19b | Horn Speaker

 Create a blend feature by sketching three sections and ensuring they each have the same number of entities.

 Check each section has the same number of entities using the sketch tools.

In this exercise, you will create the geometry for a horn speaker. You will use a three-section blend to create the base feature. One of the sections is a circle which will be divided into four entities, so that it can be blended with the four vertices of the rectangle sections. The completed part is shown in Figure 19–28.

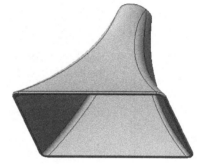

Figure 19–28

Goal | After you complete this exercise, you will be able to:

✓ **Create a three-section parallel blend**

Task 1 - Create a new part file.

1. Set the working directory to the *exercise 19b* folder.

2. Create a new part file named [horn_flare].

3. Select **Shapes > Blend** in the *Model* tab.

4. Select the Options slide-up panel and notice **Smooth** is selected by default.

5. Right-click and select **Define Internal Sketch**.

6. Select datum plane **FRONT** as the sketch plane and maintain the default orientation reference. Click Sketch .

---

7. Click ▼ next to ☐ ▼ and click ☐ (Center Rectangle). Sketch and dimension the rectangle shown in Figure 19–29.

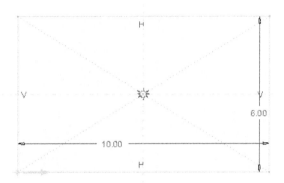

Figure 19–29

8. Click ✓ (Ok).

9. Select the Section panel and enter a depth value of [4] between the first two sections.

10. Click ☑ to create the next section.

Your start point might vary depending on how the geometry was sketched

11. Click ▼ next to ☐ ▼ and click ☐ (Center Rectangle). Sketch and dimension the rectangle shown in Figure 19–30. Verify that the start points are aligned. If the start points do not line up, select the desired location for the start point, right-click, and select **Start Point**

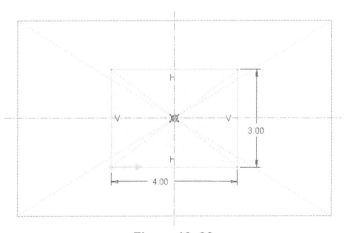

Figure 19–30

12. Click ✔ (Ok).

13. Right-click and select **Insert** to insert a third section.

14. Select the Section panel and enter a depth value of [4] between the next two sections.

15. Click 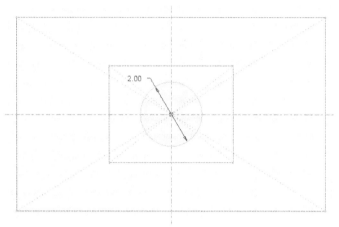 to create the third section.

16. Sketch and dimension the circle shown in Figure 19–31.

Figure 19–31

17. The first two sections contain four vertices. The circle must also be divided into four sections. Create two centerlines and constrain each one using the coincident constraint to the vertex of the large rectangle, as shown in Figure 19–32.

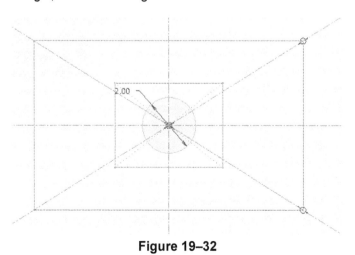

Figure 19–32

18. Click 🖛 to divide the circle into four entities. Begin with the intersection that corresponds to the start point of the rectangles, as shown in Figure 19–33.

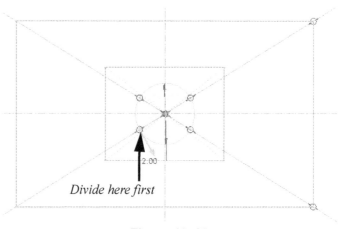

Divide here first

Figure 19–33

19. Click ✔ (OK) to exit the *Sketch* tab.

20. Complete the blend and orient the model to the Default view, as shown in Figure 19–34.

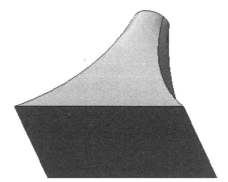

Figure 19–34

Task 2 - Create rounds.

1. Create a [0.5] radius round on the four edges shown in Figure 19–35.

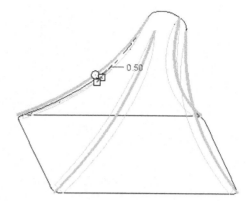

Figure 19–35

Task 3 - Shell the part.

1. Shell the part to a thickness of [0.188] and remove the two surfaces shown in Figure 19–36.

Remove the top and bottom surface

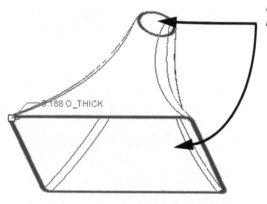

Figure 19–36

2. Create a [0.063] radius round on the edge shown in Figure 19–37.

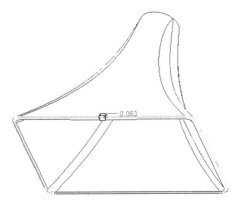

Figure 19–37

The completed part displays as shown in Figure 19–38.

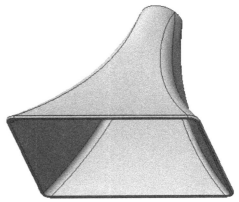

Figure 19–38

3. Save the part and erase it from memory.

Exercise 19c | (Optional) Bucket

 Create a blend feature by sketching sections and ensuring they each have the same number of entities.

 Create a bend feature using two sections.

In this exercise, you will create the part shown in Figure 19–39. It is created using two separate blend feature forms. One feature will add material as the base feature and the second will remove material. To complete the model, you will add rounds and shell the model.

Figure 19–39

Goal

After you complete this exercise, you will be able to:

✓ **Create a parallel blend feature**

Task 1 - Open a part file.

1. Set the working directory to the *exercise 19c* folder.

2. Open **bucket.prt**. The part contains a completed sketch, as shown in Figure 19–40.

Figure 19–40

3. Edit the definition of Sketch 1 to investigate the sketch geometry as shown in Figure 19–41. Note the number of entities and dimensions at the bottom of the section. This is where the spout for the bucket will be created.

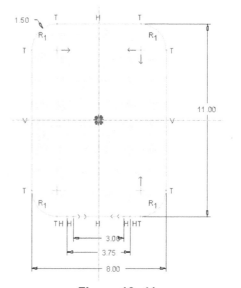

Figure 19–41

4. Click ✔ (OK) to exit Sketcher without making any changes.

Task 2 - Create a Blend feature.

1. Select **Shapes > Blend**.

2. Select the Options panel and change the blend to **Straight**.

3. Right-click and select **Define Internal Sketch**.

4. Select datum plane **Top** as the sketch plane and maintain the default orientation reference. Click **Sketch**.

5. Click ☐ to project the existing sketch as the first sub-section in the blend.

6. In the **TYPE** menu, select **Loop** as the method of selection.

7. Select any of the entities in the sketch.

8. Close the **TYPE** menu. Note that an arrow displays on the sketch, similar to that shown in Figure 19–42. This arrow is the section's start point. The start point location might vary depending on the entity selected.

Figure 19–42

9. Click ✔ (Ok).

10. Select the Sections slide-up panel and click **Insert**.

11. Enter a depth value of [6] between the first two sections.

You can also click

Sketch... *in the Sections panel.*

12. Click 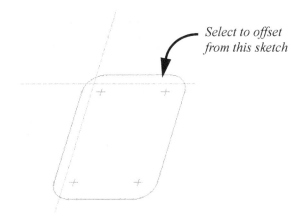 to create the next section.

13. Make sure the sketch is oriented in the default position. To sketch the second section, click ⌊⌐ in the *Sketch* tab to offset from the existing sketch.

14. Select **Loop** and select any entity on the sketch as shown in Figure 19–43.

Select to offset from this sketch

Figure 19–43

15. An arrow displays as shown in Figure 19–44, indicating the positive direction of the offset.

The arrow indicates the positive direction of the offset

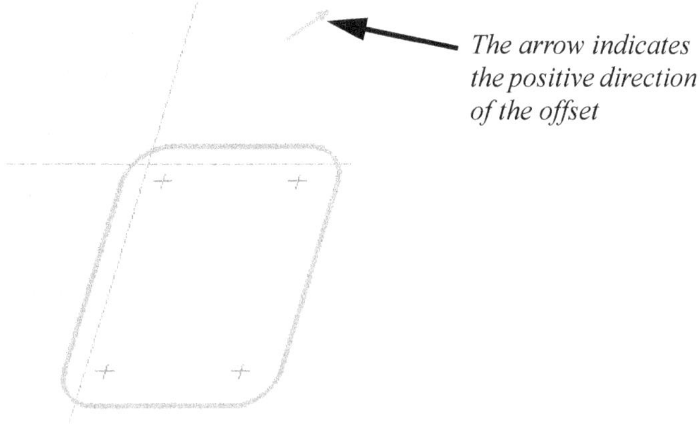

Figure 19–44

16. In the message window, enter [0.5] to create a second section that is larger than the first. Enter [-0.5] if the arrow is pointing the opposite direction. Ensure that the sketch is larger than the first section.

17. The second section's start point should be in the same position relative to the previous section's start point. If it is not, select the vertex that you want to use as the section's start point, right-click, and select **Start Point**.

18. Click  (Ok).

19. Select the Sections panel and click ⌞Insert⌟ to create a third section.

20. Select the Sections panel and enter a depth value of [0.25] between the next two sections.

21. Click ⬚ to create the next section.

22. Orient to the default view. Offset the datum curve again by a value of [0.85]. The third section should be larger than both the first and second. If necessary, correct the start point position for the section.

23. Click (Ok).

24. Insert a fourth section with a depth value of [3.00] between the two sections and offset the datum curve by a value of [1.00]. The fourth section should be larger than all of the other sections.

25. In the fourth section, you need to sketch additional geometry to create the bucket's spout. Trim away or delete the unwanted offset geometry shown in Figure 19–45.

Delete these three entities

Figure 19–45

26. Add the sketched lines and dimensions, as shown in Figure 19–46. You might also need to add a centerline and symmetry constraint to the sketch.

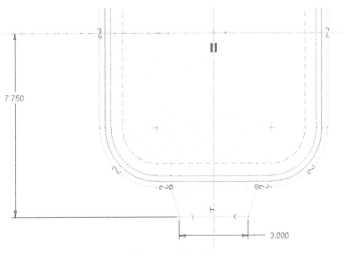

Figure 19–46

27. Complete the sketch.

28. Click 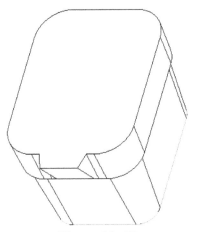 to complete the blend as shown in Figure 19–47

Figure 19–47

Task 3 - Create a blended cut to remove material from the model.

In this task, you will create an additional blend feature that removes material from the model, as shown in Figure 19–48.

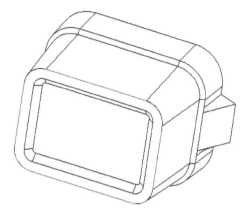

Figure 19–48

1. Select **Shapes > Blend**.

2. Click ◿ in the *Blend* tab.

3. Select **Straight** in the Options panel.

4. Right-click and select **Define Internal Sketch**.

5. Select the bottom surface of the bucket as the sketching plane and maintain the default orientation plane, as shown in Figure 19–49.

Select this surface as the sketching plane ──▶

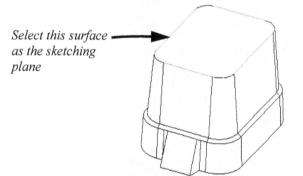

Figure 19–49

6. If necessary, select datum plane **FRONT** as the second sketcher reference. Close the References dialog box.

7. Create the first sub-section so that it is offset from the existing sketch by a distance of [0.75] (the section is smaller than the original sketch) as shown in Figure 19–50.

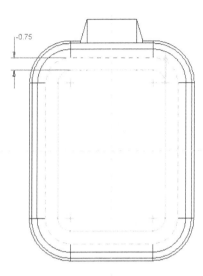

Figure 19–50

8. Click ✔ (OK)

9. Insert a second section and enter [0.5] as the depth between the sections.

Ensure you rotate the model and select the original edges to offset.

10. Click 🖉 and create the entities by offsetting from the existing sketch by a distance of [1.25] (the section is smaller than the original sketch).

11. Click ✔ (OK) to complete the sketch.

12. Click ✔ to complete the feature.

Task 4 - Create the round features.

1. Create a [0.50] radius round on the edges shown in Figure 19–51.

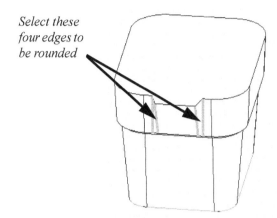

Select these four edges to be rounded

Figure 19–51

2. Create another round with a radius of [0.40] on the edge shown in Figure 19–52. All adjacent tangent edges are included in the round.

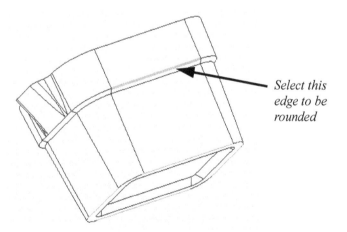

Select this edge to be rounded

Figure 19–52

3. Create another round with a radius of [0.40] on the edge as shown in Figure 19–53. All adjacent tangent edges are included in the round.

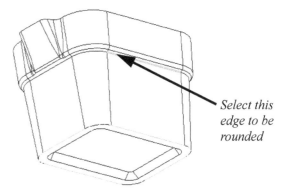

Select this edge to be rounded

Figure 19–53

4. Create a final round with a radius of [0.40] on the edges shown in Figure 19–54.

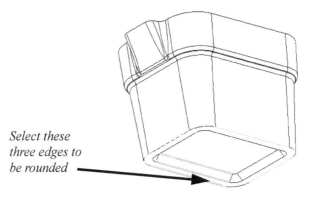

Select these three edges to be rounded

Figure 19–54

Task 5 - Create a shell feature.

1. Click 🔲 (Shell) to shell the part.

2. Select the top surface of the bucket as the surface to remove, as shown in Figure 19–55.

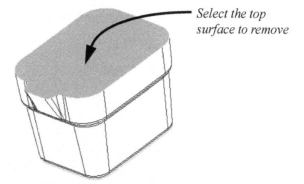

Select the top surface to remove

Figure 19–55

3. For the thickness, enter [0.125].

4. Complete the feature. The model displays as shown in Figure 19–56.

Figure 19–56

5. Save the model and close the window.

Review Questions

1. A Blend can be used in a model to add or remove material.

   a. True

   b. False

2. Which of the following statements are true regarding Parallel Blends?

   a. A Parallel Blend creates a single feature in which the geometry is blended between multiple sub-sections.

   b. A Parallel Blend can only be added to the model after the base protrusion has been created.

   c. All of the sections for a Parallel Blend are created in one sketch.

   d. A Blend Vertex is a feature similar to a Parallel Blend in that it enables you to blend geometry between selected vertices.

3. What is the minimum number of sub-sections that must exist in a Blend feature?

   a. 1

   b. 2

   c. 3

   d. There is not a minimum number of sections

4. What is the maximum number of sub-sections that can exist in a Blend feature?

   a. 2

   b. 3

   c. 100

   d. There is not a maximum number of sections

5. The sub-sections for Parallel Blends can only be sketched.

   a. True

   b. False

6. Which of the following options enables you to change a Parallel Blend that was created using the Straight option to a Smooth blend?

    a. Edit

    b. Edit References

    c. Edit Definition

    d. Value

7. Which of the following techniques enables you to change the geometry shown at the top in Figure 19–57 to that shown at the bottom in Figure 19–57?

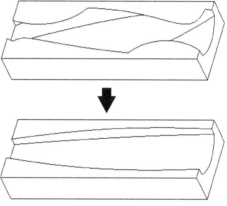

Figure 19–57

    a. Change the attributes element from *Straight* to **Smooth**.

    b. Add a **Blend Vertex** to the first sub-section in the sketch.

    c. Change the start points for each sub-section so they start in the same relative location.

    d. Create an additional sub-section with the sketch for the blend.

8. Which of the following techniques enables you to change the geometry shown on the left in Figure 19–58 to that shown on the right in Figure 19–58?

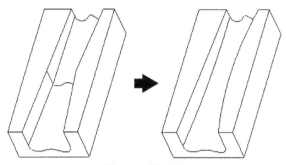

Figure 19–58

   a. Change the attributes element from *Straight* to **Smooth**.

   b. Add a **Blend Vertex** to the first sub-section in the sketch.

   c. Change the start points for each sub-section so that they start in the same relative location.

   d. Create an additional sub-section with the sketch for the blend.

9. Which of the following techniques can be used to blend a triangular sub-section that contains three entities to a circle that only contains one entity?

   a. Blend Vertex

   b. Trim tools

   c. Sketcher Point

   d. Toggle Section

10. Sections in a blend feature can be reordered.

   a. True

   b. False

Command Summary

Button	Command	Location
	Divide	• **Ribbon:** *Sketch* tab in the *Editing* group

Chapter 20

Assembly Mode

Just as features are added to one another to create a part, parts can be assembled to one another to create an assembly. The parts can be assembled individually or as members of a sub-assembly to create a higher level assembly. The parts and sub-assemblies are referred to as components.

This chapter introduces:

✓**Assembling Components**
✓**Assembly Examples**
✓**Model Tree**

Learning Objectives

This chapter provides instruction to enable you to do the following:

20.1 Assembling Components

 Insert components in an assembly.

 Locate the components in an assembly based on selected constraint type and references using the *Component Placement* tab.

 Make dimensional, constraint, or reference changes to an existing component using Edit Definition.

20.2 Assembly Examples

 Learn how to use the constraint types in the different examples provided.

20.3 Model Tree

 Open and locate components and features within an assembly using the model tree.

20.1 Assembling Components

 Insert components in an assembly.

 Locate the components in an assembly based on selected constraint type and references using the *Component Placement* tab.

 Make dimensional, constraint, or reference changes to an existing component using Edit Definition.

To create an assembly, components are inserted and constrained using the available Creo Parametric constraints. These are specified to locate components parametrically with respect to existing components and assembly features. Similar to the interdependencies between features in a part, parent/child relationships also exist within an assembly. Any references made to other components when assembling a new component create parent/child relationships.

Use the following general steps to insert a component into an assembly:

1. Insert a component.

2. Select a constraint to parametrically place the component.

3. Select the appropriate references on the assembly and component.

4. Assign an offset value, if necessary.

5. Repeat Steps 2 to 4 until the component is fully constrained.

6. Redefine the component placement, as necessary.

Step 1 - Insert a component.

To insert a component into an assembly, click (Assemble) in the Component group in the *Model* tab. In the Open dialog box, select the component to insert, and click **Open**. The *Component Placement* tab displays as shown in Figure 20–1. You can also drag a component into the assembly window from the file browser.

Figure 20–1

The tab contains the Placement and Move slide-up panels. This training guide only discusses the options for the Placement slide-up panel. The Move slide-up panel contains options for placing components non-parametrically. These are discussed in the Creo Parametric: Advanced Assembly Design and Management training guide.

The tab is the control center for the assembly process. It displays each time you assemble a new component, or redefine the placement of an existing component, and remains open throughout the placement process.

☐ and ☐ at the right side of the tab enable you to determine whether you want the component that is being assembled, to be displayed in a separate window or in the main window, respectively. By default, components are assembled in the main window. The choice should be made based on the convenience of selecting references.

Step 2 - Select a constraint to parametrically place the component.

Constraints locate components parametrically with respect to existing components or features. Constraints are assigned using the Constraint Type drop-down list in the tab or from the Placement slide-up panel, as shown in Figure 20–2.

Constraint Type drop-down lists

Figure 20–2

The available placement constraints are shown in Table 20–1.

Table 20–1

Option	Description
Automatic (default)	The system assigns an appropriate constraint type based on the references selected from the assembly and component.
Distance	Selected planar surfaces, edges, or points are constrained with an offset value. You can either drag the model using a square handle displayed on the model or enter the offset value in the Component Placement tab. The Offset value changes automatically during the dragging action.
Angle Offset	Selected planar surfaces face the same or opposite direction with an angular offset value. Specifies the rotation of a cylindrical component between two planar surfaces. You can also select lines or edges.
Parallel	Selected planer surfaces are oriented parallel. You can also select lines or edges.
Coincident	Selected planer surfaces edges face the same or opposite directions and are coplanar. Selected revolved surfaces or axes are coaxial. Selected coordinate system's axis are aligned and the origins are mated.
Normal	Selected planer surfaces are oriented perpendicular.
Coplanar	Selected planer surfaces, edges, or axis are oriented coplanar.
Centered	Selected coordinate systems are aligned.
Tangent	Selected surfaces are tangent. Surface normals face each other.
Fix	The Fix constraint fully constrains a component in its current location.
Default	The Default constraint fully constrains a component using its default coordinate system and aligns it to the assembly's default coordinate system.

As constraints are added, the menu updates to only display the remaining possible options. For example, the Default constraint is no longer available after a Coincident constraint is added.

Step 3 - Select the appropriate references on the assembly and component.

A reference to both the component and assembly are needed for each constraint. Additionally, each constraint requires its own set of placement references. For example, a Parallel constraint requires a surface or datum plane to be selected on both the component and assembly. Additional constraints are also required to fully place the component.

To display the details of the reference selection, open the Placement slide-up panel before you make any selection, as shown in Figure 20–3.

Both selection collectors are active. Therefore, you can select the component and assembly references in any order

Figure 20–3

By default, you can select component and assembly references in any order. Their status is displayed in the Placement slide-up panel, as shown in Figure 20–3.

You can specify the model for which you are selecting the reference (component or assembly) by selecting the required collector in the Placement slide-up panel. Alternatively, you can right-click and select **Select Component Item** or **Select Assembly Item** as shown in Figure 20–4, and then select the appropriate reference.

*The **Move Component** option enables you to move the new component to a more convenient position. You can also use the 3D dragger or press <Ctrl>+<Alt> simultaneously and use the mouse to reorient or move the new component.*

Figure 20–4

Once you have selected the constraint references, additional options might display. For example, when using the Coincident constraint, additional icons display in the Placement slide-up panel (**Flip**) and in the tab ( ). These enable you to flip the orientation of the component.

To change a selected reference, select the constraint in the Placement slide-up panel, select the required reference collector, and select a new reference.

*Use the **Clear** option to remove both the component and assembly references.*

Alternatively, you can change a constraint reference in the graphics window. To change a selected reference in the graphics window, select its name tag, move the cursor away from the selected name tag, right-click and select an option in the contextual menu.

Step 4 - Assign an offset value, if necessary.

The offset value can be defined before or after you have selected the constraint references.

Distance and Angle Offset constraints require you to define an offset value once the references have been selected. Offset can be defined in the Placement slide-up panel or in the tab, as shown in Figure 20–5.

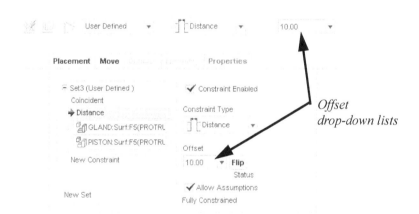

Figure 20–5

Step 5 - Repeat Steps 2 to 4 until the component is fully constrained.

Before you define the first constraint, the default status of the new component is **No Constraints**, as shown in Figure 20–6. The component displays in the View window in purple until the status indicates that the component is fully constrained or the **Allow Assumptions** are selected.

Figure 20–6

As constraints are added, the status changes to **Partially Constrained**. Finally, the status changes to **Fully Constrained** indicating that enough constraints have been defined to successfully place the component into the existing assembly. If the part or subassembly is fully constrained, the color changes from purple to orange. If you add conflicting constraints, the status changes to **Constraints Invalid**.

Adding Constraints

When constraining a component, you can select the automatic constraining default option or select your own constraints for the new component.

When using automatic constraining, the prompt: *Select any reference for auto type constraining* displays in the *Message* area. Select the assembly and component references to constrain the component. Creo Parametric automatically assigns the appropriate constraint type and adds each new constraint to the Placement slide-up panel.

You can also select the constraint type in the tab or in the Placement slide-up panel. In this case, Creo Parametric knows which constraint you want to create and prompts you to select the appropriate references. Once you have finished defining a constraint, Creo Parametric activates the automatic constraining again. To add another constraint, select the **New Constraint** option in the Placement slide-up panel, as shown in Figure 20–7.

*You can also right-click and select **New Constraint**.*

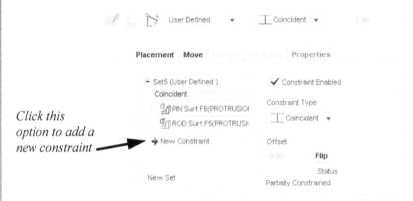

Click this option to add a new constraint

Figure 20–7

Component placement are not always in the required orientation because Creo Parametric makes assumptions. You can prevent this by clearing the **Allow Assumptions** option, as shown in Figure 20–8. The option is toggled on by default.

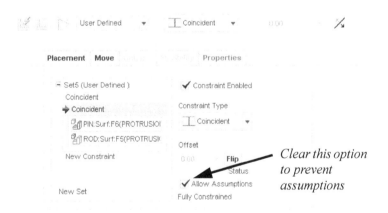

Clear this option to prevent assumptions

Figure 20–8

Deleting Constraints

To delete a constraint, select it in the Placement slide-up panel, right-click, and select **Delete**.

You can also delete a constraint by selecting its name tag in the graphics window, right-clicking, and selecting **Delete**.

Step 6 - Redefine the component placement, as necessary.

The placement of a component can be redefined by selecting it, right-clicking, and selecting **Edit Definition**. The Component Placement tab displays. In the Placement slide-up panel, all of the constraints used to place the component are displayed. The constraint type, component references, and assembly references can be changed or removed. As each constraint is selected in the Placement slide-up panel, the corresponding assembly and component references highlight on the model. To differentiate between the assembly and component references, hover the cursor over the reference's collector. The reference is pre-highlighted on the model.

20.2 Assembly Examples

Learn how to use the constraint types in the different examples provided.

The following four examples use different combinations of constraints and references to create four different assemblies. The components to be placed are shown in Figure 20–9.

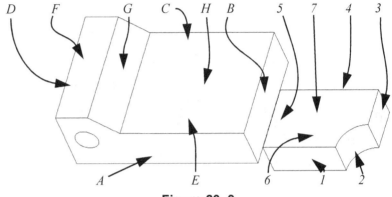

Figure 20–9

Example 1: Coincident

The combination of constraints and references listed in Table 20–2 are used to create the assembly shown in Figure 20–10.

Table 20–2

Constraint	References
Coincident	Surfaces 7 and H
Coincident	Surfaces 5 and A
Coincident	Surfaces 4 and B

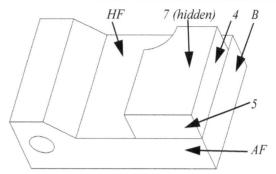

Figure 20–10

Example 2: Distance and Coincident

The combination of constraints and references listed in Table 20–3 are used to create the assembly shown in Figure 20–11.

Table 20–3

Constraint	References
Distance	Surfaces 7 and H
Coincident	Surfaces 5 and A
Coincident	Surfaces 4 and B

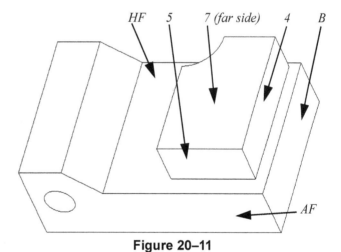

Figure 20–11

Example 3: Coincident

The combination of constraints and references listed in Table 20–4 are used to create the assembly shown in Figure 20–12.

Table 20–4

Constraint	References
Coincident	Surfaces 6 and H
Coincident	Surfaces 5 and B
Coincident	Surfaces 4 and A

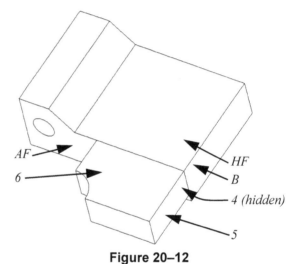

Figure 20–12

Example 4: Distance and Coincident

The combination of constraints and references listed in Table 20–5 are used to create the assembly shown in Figure 20–13.

Table 20–5

Constraint	References
Distance	Surfaces 5 and B
Coincident	Surfaces 6 and H
Coincident	Surfaces 4 and A

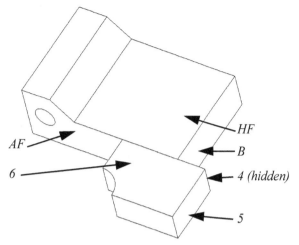

Figure 20–13

Example 5: Coincident

Examples 5 and 6 use different combinations of constraints to create the same assembly. The components to be placed are shown in Figure 20–14.

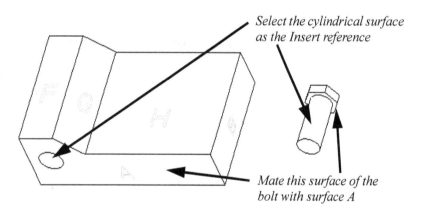

Select the cylindrical surface as the Insert reference

Mate this surface of the bolt with surface A

Figure 20–14

The combination of constraints and references listed in Table 20–6 are used the create the assembly shown in Figure 20–15.

Table 20–6

Constraint	References
Coincident	The cylindrical surface of the bolt and the cylindrical surface created by the hole.
Coincident	The bottom surface of the bolt head and surface A.

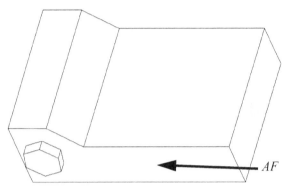

Figure 20–15

Example 6: Coincident and Parallel

The combination of constraints and references listed in Table 20–7 can be used to create the same assembly, as shown in Figure 20–16.

Table 20–7

Constraint	References
Coincident	The cylindrical surface of the bolt and the cylindrical surface created by the hole.
Coincident	The bottom surface of the bolt head and surface A.
Parallel	Surface X of the bolt and surface B.

The first two constraints fully define the placement. However, Parallel is used to define the orientation of the bolt. You could also use Align Angle.

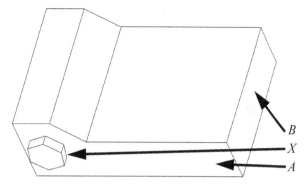

Figure 20–16

Example 7: Tangent and Coincident

Examples 7 and 8 show that using two different combinations of constraints can make a difference in the resulting assembly. The components to be placed are shown in Figure 20–17.

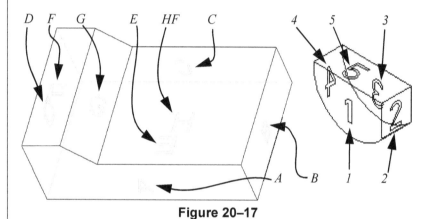

Figure 20–17

The combination of constraints and references listed in Table 20–8 are used to create the assembly shown in Figure 20–18.

Table 20–8

Constraint	References
Tangent	Surfaces G and 4
Parallel	Surfaces B and 2
Coincident	Surfaces A and 1
Tangent	Surfaces H and 4

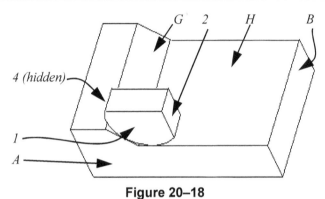

Figure 20–18

Example 8: Tangent, Parallel and Coincident

The combination of constraints and references listed in Table 20–9 are used to create the assembly shown in Figure 20–19.

Table 20–9

Constraint	References
Coincident	Surface H and Edge 4-2
Tangent	Surfaces G and 4
Coincident	Surfaces A and 1
Parallel	Surfaces G and 5

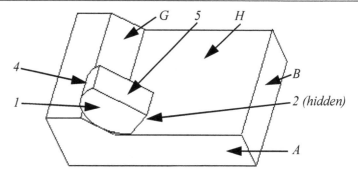

Figure 20–19

Example 9: Default or Centered

As shown in the previous examples, more than one constraint must be used to fully define how components are to be assembled. However, the Default constraint can be used alone. The following example uses the Default constraints listed in Table 20–10, to place the components shown in Figure 20–20. The resulting assembly displays as shown in Figure 20–21.

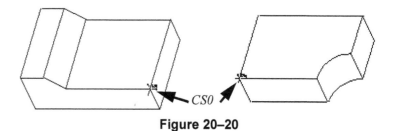

Figure 20–20

Table 20–10

Constraint	References
Default	CS0 & CS0

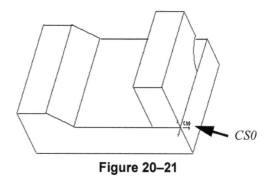

Figure 20–21

20.3 Model Tree

 Open and locate components and features within an assembly using the model tree.

The model tree lists all of the parts and sub-assemblies that make up an assembly. You can manipulate parts directly in the model tree (e.g., **Open** or **Edit**). To open a component of an assembly, select it in the model tree, right-click, and select **Open**. The part or sub-assembly opens in a separate window.

To expand the tree and display the components of a sub-assembly, select the plus ( ) symbol next to the assembly name. To compress the expanded section, select the minus ( ) symbol, as shown in Figure 20–22.

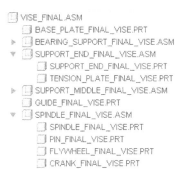

Figure 20–22

Click and **Tree Filters** in the Navigator window and select the **Features** option in the *Display* area in the Model Tree Items dialog box to see the assembly and part features in the model tree, as shown in Figure 20–23.

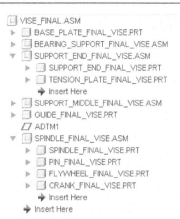

Figure 20–23

Click 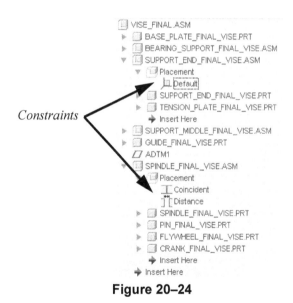 >**Tree Filters** in the Navigator window. In the Model Tree Items dialog box, in the *Display* area, select the **Placement Folder** option to see the assembly constraints in the model tree, as shown in Figure 20–24.

Constraints

Figure 20–24

Exercise 20a | Assembly Basics I

 Insert components in an assembly.

 Locate components in an assembly based on selected constraint type and references using the *Component Placement* tab.

 Make dimensional, constraint, or reference changes on an existing component using Edit Definition.

In this exercise, you will open the existing assembly shown in Figure 20–25 and assemble additional components. The following tasks and steps for the assembly constraints reference the lettered and numbered sides on the components. Add and remove constraints as needed to reach the required design intent. In addition, redefine the original constraints and references and make modifications to the assembly dimensions.

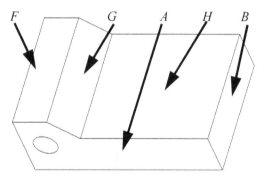

Figure 20–25

Goal After you complete this exercise, you will be able to:

- ✓ **Constrain components in an assembly**
- ✓ **Edit component placements**
- ✓ **Modify assembly dimensions**

Task 1 - Change the working directory and open an assembly file.

1. Set the working directory to the *exercise 20a* folder.

2. Open **practice.asm**. Toggle off the display of the datum planes and coordinate systems, if they are currently displayed.

Task 2 - Assemble the part named bblock.prt.

1. Click 🔳 (Assemble) in the Component group in the *Model* tab.

2. In the Open dialog box, select **bblock.prt**, and click `Open ▼`.
   The *Component Placement* tab displays. The new component

   displays in the main window because 🔲 is activated by default.

You can also move the component using <Ctrl>+ <Alt> and the mouse to orient the component. Click and hold the right mouse button to pan the component, or click and hold the middle mouse button to spin the component.

3. The component is displayed in the main window along with the 3D dragger as shown in Figure 20–26. Note that the color of the added component is purple. Drag the centerpoint of the 3D dragger to freely move the component.

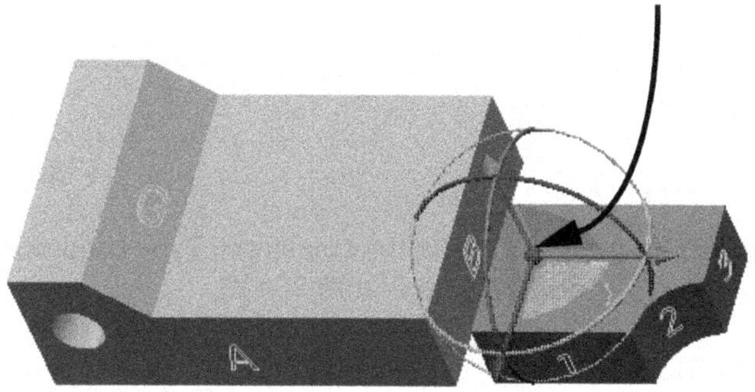

Drag the center to move the component

Figure 20–26

4. Drag an arrow to translate the component along the axis.

5. Select a rotation arc to rotate the component.

6. Open the Placement slide-up panel and leave it open during the assembly process.

Task 3 - Define the first constraint.

The first constraint is coincident to mate surface 6 on **bblock.prt** and surface H on **ablock.prt** (which is already in **practice.asm**), as shown in Figure 20–27.

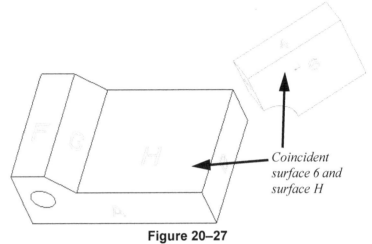

Coincident surface 6 and surface H

Figure 20–27

The 3D dragger can be turned off by clicking ⊕ in the Component Placement tab.

1. In the Constraint Type drop-down list, select **Coincident** as shown in Figure 20–28.

Figure 20–28

2. In **bblock.prt**, select surface **6**.

3. In **ablock.prt**, select surface **H**.

4. Note that the green axis on the 3D dragger displays in gray indicating that the model can no longer move in that direction. Look at the *Component Placement* tab. The STATUS now displays as **Partially Constrained**. The first constraint has been added and the second can now be defined.

5. Surface 6 and surface H should be facing opposite directions. If the surfaces are facing the same direction, click ⚞ in the *Component Placement* tab, to flip the part.

Task 4 - Define a second constraint.

The second constraint uses coincident to align surface 3 on **bblock.prt** and surface B on **ablock.prt**, as shown in Figure 20–29.

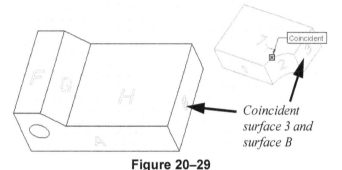

Coincident surface 3 and surface B

Figure 20–29

1. Right-click and select **New Constraint**.

2. In the Constraint Type drop-down list, select **Coincident**.

3. In **bblock.prt**, select surface **3**.

4. In **ablock.prt**, select surface **B**.

5. Look at the *Component Placement* tab. The STATUS still displays as **Partially Constrained**. With the current constraints, **bblock.prt** can still lie anywhere on surface H while remaining aligned to surface B. A third constraint is required to fully constrain the part.

Task 5 - Define a third constraint.

The third constraint uses coincident to align surface 1 on **bblock.prt** and surface A on **ablock.prt**, as shown in Figure 20–30.

Coincident constraint for surface 1 and surface A

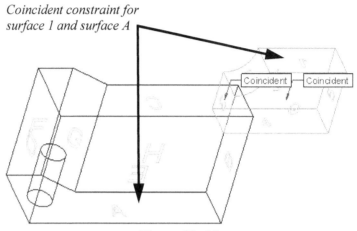

Figure 20–30

1. Right-click and select **New Constraint**.

2. In the Constraint Type drop-down list, select **Coincident**.

3. In **bblock.prt**, select surface **1**.

4. In **ablock.prt**, select surface **A**.

5. Creo Parametric might create the constraint but place the part in the opposite direction. If so, click in the *Component Placement* tab, to flip the part.

6. Look at the *Component Placement* tab. The STATUS now displays as **Fully Constrained**.

Task 6 - Check the placement of the component in the assembly.

1. Check the placement of **bblock.prt** in the assembly. It must correspond to Figure 20–31.

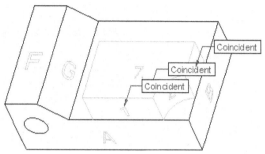

Figure 20–31

2. If the component does not display as expected, click ✖ and repeat the previous steps. If the placement is correct, click ✔.

Task 7 - Assemble bblock.prt a second time.

Assemble **bblock.prt** a second time as shown in Figure 20–32.

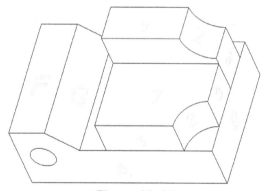

Figure 20–32

1. Click 📐 (Assemble) and select **bblock.prt** as the component to be assembled.

2. Open the Placement slide-up panel and leave it open during the assembly process.

3. Select **Coincident** for surfaces **4** and **H** as shown in Figure 20–33.

4. Right-click and select **New Constraint**.

5. Select **Coincident** for surfaces **6** and **4** as shown in Figure 20–33.

6. Right-click and select **New Constraint**.

7. Select **Coincident** for surface **3** and **B** as shown in Figure 20–33.

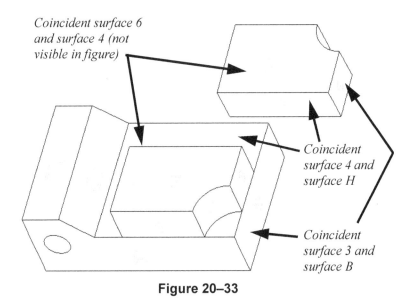

Coincident surface 6 and surface 4 (not visible in figure)

Coincident surface 4 and surface H

Coincident surface 3 and surface B

Figure 20–33

8. Click ✔ to finish the placing the component.

Task 8 - Assemble the part called pin.prt.

---

1. Click 🔧 (Assemble) and select **pin.prt** as the component to be assembled.

2. Open the Placement slide-up panel and leave it open during the assembly process.

You can also use the 3D dragger to move the component.

3. Before you start assembling, press <Ctrl>+<Alt> and use the mouse to orient the component to a more appropriate position. Press and hold the right mouse button to pan the component, Press and hold the middle mouse button to spin the component.

4. Assemble the component as shown in Figure 20–34. The assembled component displays as shown in Figure 20–35.

If the parallel constraint is your third constraint, you might need to clear the **Allow Assumptions** *option in the Placement slide-up panel to be able to add this constraint. This is because the first two constraints are sufficient to place the component and the orientation of surface X is assumed by the system. Even though the assumption might be correct, you can add the final constraint to ensure that the surfaces remain oriented regardless of changes that might be made to the models.*

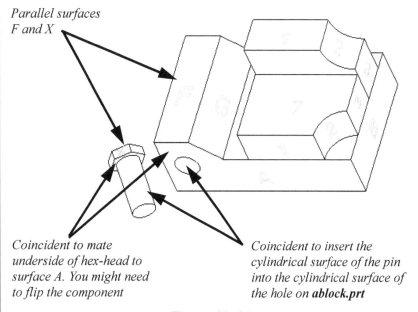

Parallel surfaces F and X

Coincident to mate underside of hex-head to surface A. You might need to flip the component

Coincident to insert the cylindrical surface of the pin into the cylindrical surface of the hole on **ablock.prt**

Figure 20–34

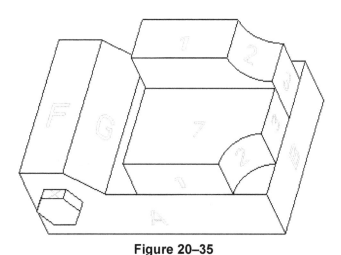

Figure 20–35

Task 9 - Assemble additional instances of ablock.prt and bblock.prt.

1. Assemble the two additional instances of **ablock.prt** and **bblock.prt**, as shown in Figure 20–36.

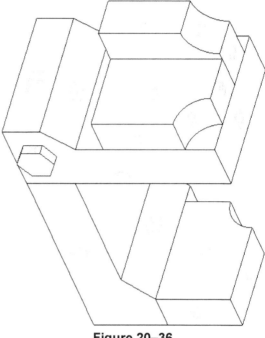

Figure 20–36

Task 10 - Edit the definition of the second instance of ablock.prt in the assembly.

*To easily select the model in the main window, select **Parts** in the filter at the bottom of the main assembly window.*

1. Select the second instance of **ablock.prt** in the model tree or in the model. Right-click and select **Edit Definition**. The original *Component Placement* tab that was used to assemble the component displays.

2. Open the Placement slide-up panel and leave it open during the assembly process.

*You can also select the name tags of the Align constraints directly on the model, right-click, and select **Delete**.*

3. Find and remove the appropriate two Coincident constraints. Select them in the Placement slide-up panel, right-click, and select **Delete**.

4. Add two new constraints to position the component, as shown in Figure 20–37.

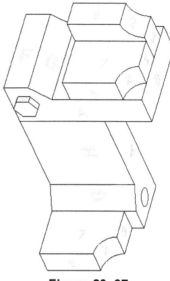

Figure 20–37

5. Click 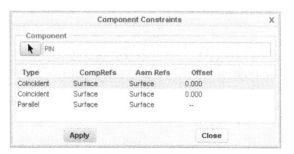 to complete the redefinition of the assembly. The **bblock.prt** component updates relative to the new location for **bblock.prt** because of its placement references.

Task 11 - Obtain information on component placement.

1. Select the *Tools* tab and click (Component).

2. Select **pin.prt** in the model tree or on the model. An expanded Component Constraints dialog box opens as shown in Figure 20–38. The constraints displays in the order in which you added them.

*To easily select the model in the main window, select **Parts** in the selection filter at the bottom of the main assembly window.*

Component Constraints ✕

Component

PIN

Type	CompRefs	Asm Refs	Offset
Coincident	Surface	Surface	0.000
Coincident	Surface	Surface	0.000
Parallel	Surface	Surface	--

Apply   Close

Figure 20–38

3. Select each constraint listed in the dialog box. As you do, note that it highlights the reference surfaces on the model.

4. Click **Apply**. The browser window opens with additional information about the component. The information is written to a text file called **pin.memb**, which is stored in the current working directory.

5. Close both the browser window and Component Constraints dialog box.

Task 12 - Delete all components except for the base component.

---

1. Delete all of the components except the first instance of **ablock.prt**. Remember that parent/child relationships exist. For example, you cannot delete the second instance of **ablock.prt** without the Delete dialog box opening indicating that a child must also be considered.

Task 13 - Assemble bblock.prt using the Align offset.

You can drag the component to the appropriate position before you enter the exact offset value, using the 3D dragger or by pressing <Ctrl>+<Alt> simultaneously and using the mouse to orient it.

1. Assemble **bblock.prt** using a two coincident constraints and a Distance constraint with a value of [1.0] between surfaces 6 and A, as shown in Figure 20–39. You might need to use an offset of [-1.0] to change the offset direction.

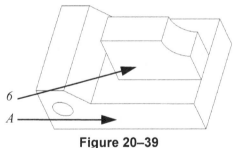

Figure 20–39

Task 14 - Modify the offset value of bblock.prt.

---

*To easily select the model in the main window, select **Parts** in the selection filter at the bottom of the main assembly window.*

1. Select **bblock.prt** in the model tree or on the model. Right-click and select **Edit**.

2. Select the offset dimension and enter [2].

3. Click 🔄 to regenerate the model.

4. Save the assembly and erase all of the models from memory.

Exercise 20b | Motor Frame

 Insert components in an assembly.

 Locate components in an assembly based on selected constraint type and references using the *Component Placement* tab.

 Make dimensional, constraint or reference changes on an existing component using Edit Definition.

In this exercise, you will open an existing assembly and assemble a subassembly. You will then continue assembling components to complete the top-level assembly. The completed assembly is shown in Figure 20–40.

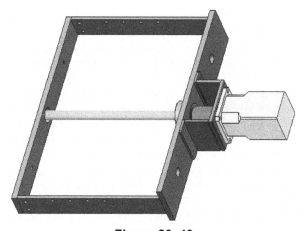

Figure 20–40

Goal | After you complete this exercise, you will be able to:

✓ **Assemble a subassembly**
✓ **Assemble parts to complete the top-level assembly**

Task 1 - Change the working directory and open an assembly file.

1. Set the working directory to the *exercise 20b* folder.

2. Open **motor_frame.asm**. The assembly displays as shown in Figure 20–41.

Figure 20–41

Task 2 - Assemble a subassembly.

1. Click 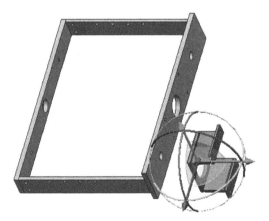 (Assemble) in the *Model* tab.

2. Select **motor_mount.asm** as the file to assemble. The assembly displays as shown in Figure 20–42.

Figure 20–42

3. Open the Placement slide-up panel and leave it open during the assembly process. Click ⊕⃗ to turn off the 3D dragger.

By default, the new component displays in the main window because 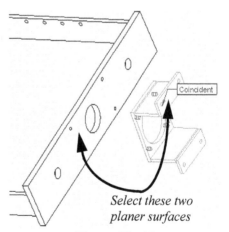 is activated.

Task 3 - Define the first constraint.

1. Select the two circular surfaces shown in Figure 20–43. Ensure that **Coincident** is the type of constraint being used.

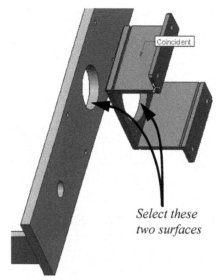

Select these two surfaces

Figure 20–43

Task 4 - Define the second constraint.

1. Right-click and select **New Constraint**. Select the two surfaces shown in Figure 20–44.

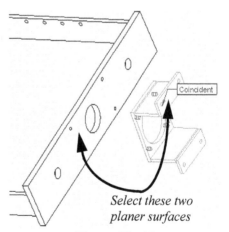

Select these two planer surfaces

Figure 20–44

2. Ensure that Coincident is the type of constraint being used. The model updates to displays as shown in Figure 20–45. Click 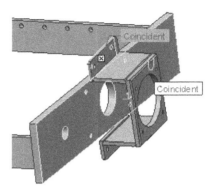 in the *Component Placement* tab, if necessary.

Figure 20–45

Task 5 - Define a third constraint.

1. Right-click and select **New Constraint**.

2. Select the two bolt hole surfaces shown in Figure 20–46. Ensure Coincident is the type of constraint being used.

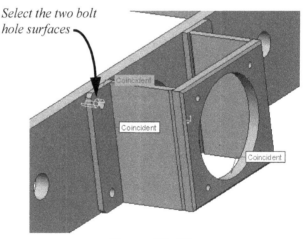

Figure 20–46

3. Look at the *Component Placement* tab. The STATUS now displays

   as **Fully Constrained**. Click ✓ to complete the component
   placement, as shown in Figure 20–47.

Figure 20–47

Task 6 - Assemble the electric motor part.

1. Assemble **motor.prt**.

2. Before you add constraints, use the 3D dragger or press <Ctrl>+
   <Alt> and use the left, middle, and right mouse buttons to reorient
   the component to a more appropriate position, as shown in
   Figure 20–48.

Figure 20–48

---

3. Create a Coincident constraint and select the two cylindrical surfaces, as shown in Figure 20–49.

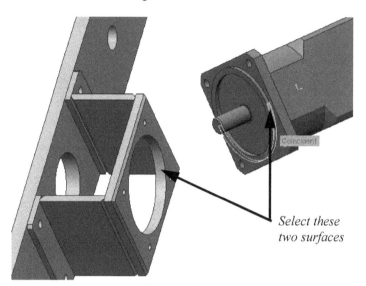

Select these two surfaces

Figure 20–49

4. Apply a Coincident constraint and pick the two planer surfaces, as shown in Figure 20–50.

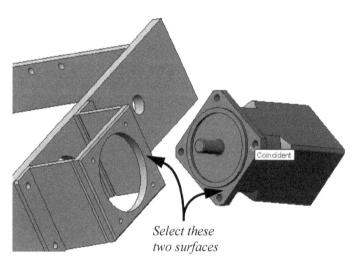

Select these two surfaces

Figure 20–50

5. Create a Coincident constraint as shown in Figure 20–51.

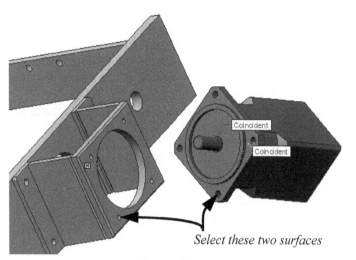

Select these two surfaces

Figure 20–51

The motor part is fully constrained, as shown in Figure 20–52.

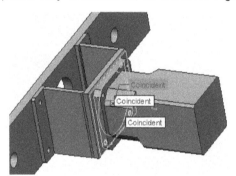

Figure 20–52

6. Click ✓ to complete the component placement.

Task 7 - Assemble the bearing housing part.

1. Assemble **bearing_housing.prt**. Use a Coincident constraint to align the cylindrical surfaces. Use a second Coincident constraint to mate the small surface of the bearing housing part to the surface of the frame, as shown in Figure 20–53.

Select the small surface of the bearing housing part and the surface of the frame

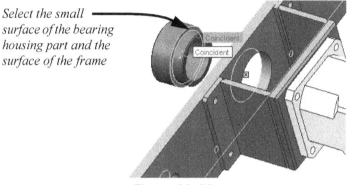

Figure 20–53

The constrained bearing housing part displays as shown in Figure 20–54.

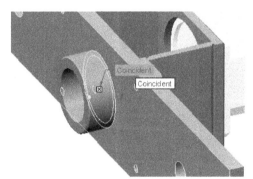

Figure 20–54

2. Complete the component placement.

Task 8 - Assemble the bearing part.

1. Assemble **bearing.prt** as shown in Figure 20–55. Add a
   Coincident constraint to align the surfaces. Add a second
   Coincident constraint to insert the cylindrical surface.

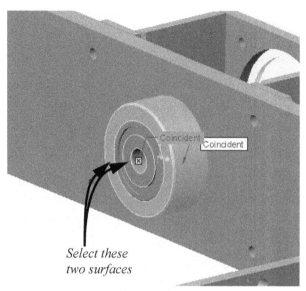

*Select these
two surfaces*

Figure 20–55

Task 9 - Assemble the shaft part.

1. Assemble **shaft.prt** using a Coincident constraint, as shown in
   Figure 20–56.

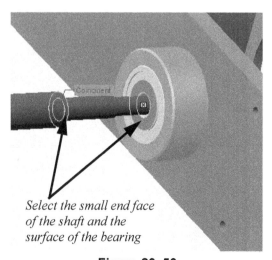

*Select the small end face
of the shaft and the
surface of the bearing*

Figure 20–56

2. Add a second coincident constrain and select the two cylindrical surfaces to fully constrain the components. The constrained shaft displays as shown in Figure 20–57.

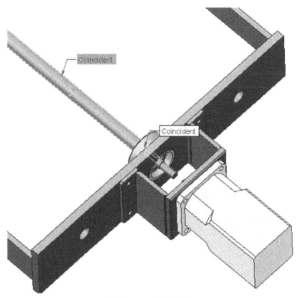

Figure 20–57

Task 10 - Assemble the coupling part.

1. Assemble **coupling.prt** using two Coincident constraints, as shown in Figure 20–58.

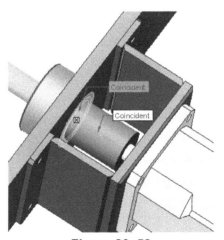

Figure 20–58

The completed assembly displays as shown in Figure 20–59.

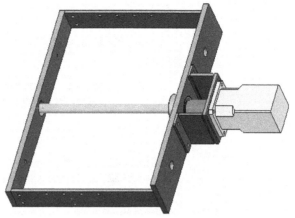

Figure 20–59

2. Save the assembly and erase it from memory.

Exercise 20c | Subassemblies (Optional)

 Insert subassemblies in an assembly.

 Locate subassemblies in an assembly based on selected constraint type and references using the *Component Placement* tab.

In this exercise, you will create an assembly by assembling parts and assemblies, and then assemble it into a top-level assembly.

Goal After you complete this exercise, you will be able to:

✓ **Assemble subassemblies**

Task 1 - Change the working directory and open an assembly file.

1. Set the working directory to the *exercise 20c* folder.

2. Open **rod.asm**. The assembly displays as shown in Figure 20–60. It currently only contains the base component, **rod**.

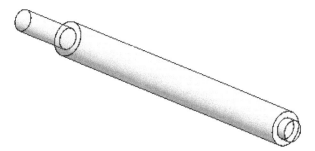

Figure 20–60

Task 2 - Assemble a subassembly.

1. Assemble **piston.asm** as shown in Figure 20–61.

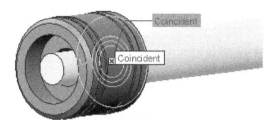

Figure 20–61

2. Assemble **washer.prt** as shown in Figure 20–62.

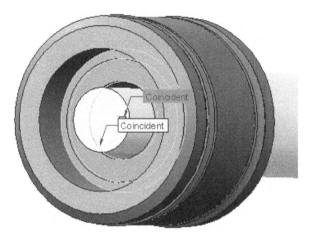

Figure 20–62

3. Assemble **nut.prt** as shown in Figure 20–63.

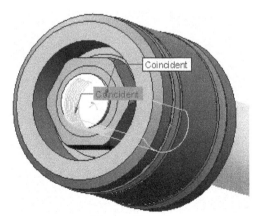

Figure 20–63

4. Assemble **gland.asm** as shown in Figure 20–64.

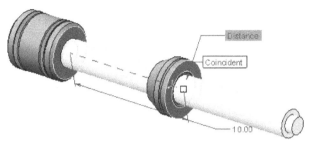

Figure 20–64

5. Save the assembly.

Task 3 - Open the top-level assembly.

1. Open **cylinder.asm**. The assembly has a base component assembled, as shown in Figure 20–65.

Figure 20–65

2. Assemble the **rod.asm** that you just created into **cylinder.asm**, as shown in Figure 20–66.

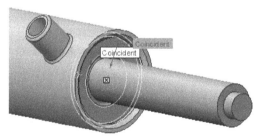

Figure 20–66

Ensure that the Coincident constraint references the front face of the gland part and the aft face of the groove in the barrel part, as shown in Figure 20–67.

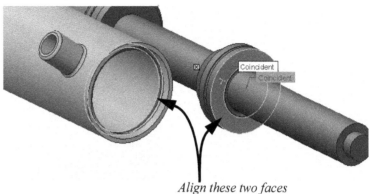

Align these two faces

Figure 20–67

3. Assemble **clevis.prt** as shown in Figure 20–68.

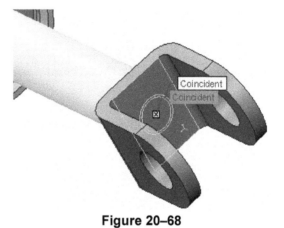

Figure 20–68

4. Assemble **retaining_ring.prt** as shown in Figure 20–69. Ensure that the Coincident constraint references the outside diameter of the retaining ring and the surface of the groove.

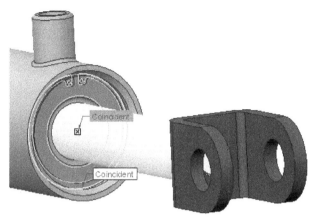

Figure 20–69

The completed assembly displays as shown in Figure 20–70.

Figure 20–70

5. Save the assembly and erase it from memory.

Review Questions

1. Parent/child relationships cannot exist between components in an assembly.

    a. True

    b. False

2. Which of the following icons enables you to assemble a component into an assembly?

    a.

    b.

    c.

    d.

3. In the *Component Placement* tab, which of the following icons enables you to assemble a new component while remaining in the main assembly window?

    a.

    b.

    c.

    d.

4. Which of the following are valid constraint types that can be used to assemble components into an assembly? (Select all that apply.)

    a. Coincident

    b. Distance

    c. Tangent

    d. Tangent to Pnt

5. What is the minimum number of constraints that can be used to parametrically locate a component in an assembly?

   a. 0

   b. 1

   c. 3

   d. 4

6. Which of the following constraint options enable you to constrain a component so that two surfaces are aligned but you still maintain the flexibility of entering an offset value if the design intent changes?

   a. Distance

   b. Parallel

   c. Coincident

7. The *Assembly item* collector in the Placement slide-up panel in the Component Placement tab enables you to define the reference for the component that is being assembled into the assembly.

   a. True

   b. False

8. Which of the following statements are true when you use the Coincident constraint for two planar surfaces? (Select all that apply.)

   a. The surface normals point in the same direction.

   b. Constraining two surfaces to be Coincident is equivalent to using the Distant constraint with a value of 0.

   c. The surface normals point in opposite directions.

   d. Equivalent to using the Normal constraint.

9. Which of the assemblies shown in could have used the Parallel constraint to constrain surfaces C and 2 and surfaces A and 3?

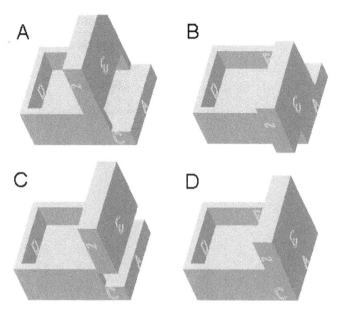

A B

C D

Figure 20–71

a. A

b. B

c. C

d. D

Command Summary

Button	Command	Location
	Assemble	• **Ribbon:** *Model* tab in the *Component* group
	Settings	• Model Tree

Chapter 21

Assembly Tools

In the previous chapter, you learned that components are constrained to one another to form assemblies. The constraints that you use result in parent/child relationships between the components. In this chapter, you learn to assemble components using datum planes as references; this technique avoids unwanted parent/child relationships. You also learn a number of other tools that can be used while in Assembly mode to evaluate and review the entire assembly.

This chapter introduces:

✓**Assembly with Datum Planes**

✓**Editing an Assembly and its Components**

✓**Exploded Views**

✓**Interference Checks**

✓**Bill of Materials**

✓**Assembly Layers**

Learning Objectives

This chapter provides instruction to enable you to do the following:

21.1 Assembly with Datum Planes

 Locate components in an assembly using the datum planes and axis as constraint references.

21.2 Editing an Assembly and its Components

 Edit existing components within an assembly using proper editing tools.

21.3 Exploded Views

 Customize and create exploded views using the View Manager dialog box.

21.4 Interference Checks

 Check for interference between the components of the assembly using the Global Interference Analysis command.

21.5 Bill of Materials

 Generate a bill of materials for the assembly to determine what components are used and how often.

21.6 Assembly Layers

 Hide, unhide, and isolate layers using the layer tree in an assembly.

21.1 Assembly with Datum Planes

 Locate components in an assembly using the datum planes and axis as constraint references.

As with new parts, new assemblies should start with default datum planes. Using default datum planes makes the assembly more robust. They enable you to easily perform operations, such as patterning and reordering components.

Default datum planes are provided with all standard assembly templates. They can also be created as the first features in the assembly by clicking ▱ (Plane) in the Datum group in the *Model* tab. Default datum planes created using the default template are named ASM_RIGHT, ASM_TOP, and ASM_FRONT, as shown in Figure 21–1. However, default datum planes created within the assembly model are named ADTM1, ADTM2, and ADTM3.

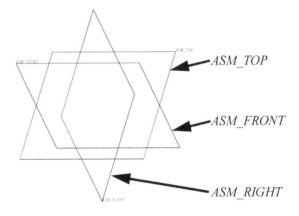

Figure 21–1

Datum planes can be used as constraint references when defining component placements. When a datum plane is selected as a reference, you can click ⤢ in the *Component Placement* tab or click

Flip in the Placement slide-up panel to flip the component into the proper orientation if the default is not acceptable. When a datum plane is selected, the action is applied to its dominant (brown) side by default.

In the example in Figure 21–2, the bracket part shown on the right is assembled to the assembly's default datum planes (shown on the left), using the selected constraints.

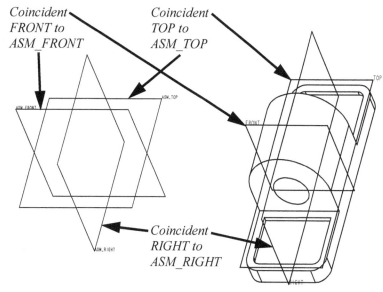

*Coincident
FRONT to
ASM_FRONT*

*Coincident
TOP to
ASM_TOP*

*Coincident
RIGHT to
ASM_RIGHT*

Figure 21–2

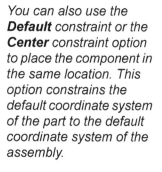

*You can also use the **Default** constraint or the **Center** constraint option to place the component in the same location. This option constrains the default coordinate system of the part to the default coordinate system of the assembly.*

To create this assembly, datum plane RIGHT is constrained to datum plane ASM_RIGHT of the assembly using Coincident. This forces datum planes RIGHT and ASM_RIGHT to be coplanar and face the same direction. Likewise, datum plane TOP is constrained to datum plane ASM_TOP, and datum plane FRONT is constrained to ASM_FRONT using Coincident. These three constraints are sufficient to fully constrain the part on the assembly's default datum planes, as shown in Figure 21–3.

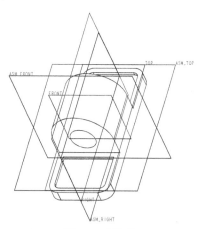

Figure 21–3

Next the pin part is assembled, as shown in Figure 21–4. The following three constraints are used:

- Coincident is used to constrain axis A_1 of the pin to axis A_1 of the bracket.
- Coincident is used to constrain datum plane FRONT of the pin to datum plane ASM_FRONT of the assembly.
- Parallel is used to constrain datum plane TOP of the pin to datum plane ASM_TOP of the assembly.

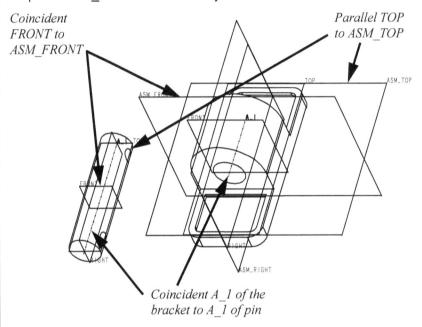

Coincident FRONT to ASM_FRONT

Parallel TOP to ASM_TOP

Coincident A_1 of the bracket to A_1 of pin

Figure 21–4

The pin can then be placed, as shown in Figure 21–5.

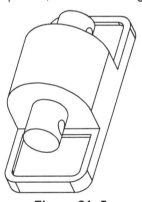

Figure 21–5

The pin is a child of the bracket because the datum axis of the pin to the datum axis of the bracket are constrained. Both components are children of the assembly's default datum planes.

Finally, the U-hook part is assembled, as shown in Figure 21–6. The following three constraints are used:

- Coincident is used to constrain datum plane RIGHT of the U-hook to datum plane ASM_FRONT of the assembly.
- Coincident is used to constrain datum plane TOP of the U-hook to datum plane ASM_RIGHT of the assembly.
- Coincident is used to constrain axis A_2 of the U-hook to axis A_1 of the bracket.

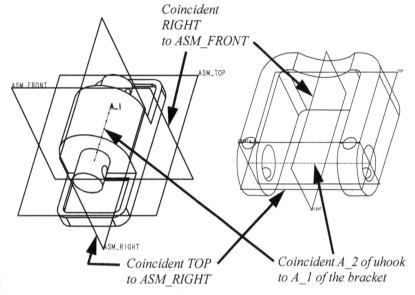

Figure 21–6

The U-hook can then be placed, as shown in Figure 21–7.

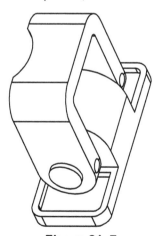

Figure 21–7

Axis A_2 of the U-hook could have been constrained to axis A_1 of the pin instead of axis A_1 of the bracket. Which axis to select would depend on the design intent. Remember that assembly constraints result in parent/child relationships. Consider the following scenarios:

Case 1

A variety of pin parts could be used with this assembly. In each case, the U-hook and bracket parts would remain the same. If the axis of the U-hook was constrained to the axis of the pin, you would need to use the **Edit Definition** or **Edit References** option if the pin component was deleted. This is because the U-hook would be a child of the pin. In this situation, it would be better to constrain the axis of the U-hook to the axis of the bracket.

Case 2

Again, a variety of different pin parts could be used with this assembly. However, this time there is a corresponding U-hook for each pin. If the pin was deleted, you would also need to delete the U-hook. In this situation, you would want to have the U-hook as a child of the pin so that they could be deleted together easily.

21.2 Editing an Assembly and its Components

 Edit existing components within an assembly using the editing tools.

Several options can be used to make changes to an assembly and its components. These include the following:

- To make changes to an assembly you can use the **Edit**, **Edit Definition,** and **Edit References** options found in the menu bar or in contextual menu. These options enable you to make changes to the dimension values, constraints, and references, respectively.

- To make changes to a component while in Assembly mode, you must first activate the component. You can select it in the model tree or directly on the model, right-click, and select **Activate**. This option activates the Part mode options and tabs so that you can make changes to the assembly component while still in Assembly mode. Once a component is activated, the model tree and main window update, as shown in Figure 21–8.

*Click ⚒ ▾ and **Tree Filters** in the Navigator window and select the **Features** option in the Display area in the Model Tree Items dialog box to display the assembly and part features in the model tree.*

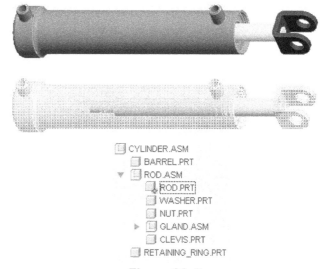

Figure 21–8

21.3 Exploded Views

 Customize and create exploded views using the View Manager dialog box.

Creo Parametric enables you to create exploded views of assemblies. By customizing the exploded positions of the components, you can create a view that can be used in a drawing to indicate an assembly procedure.

To create a customized explode click ⬛ (Manage Views) in the Model Display group in the *Model* tab or in the Graphics toolbar and then select the *Explode* tab, as shown in Figure 21–9.

To create a temporary explode, click ⬛ in the Model Display group in the Model tab. The model displays in its default exploded position and can be modified by dynamically dragging components to new positions in the view. Click the icon again to revert the assembly back to its assembled state.

View Manager			✕
Simp Rep	Style		Xsec
Layers	**Explode**	Orient	All

New Edit ▾ ⬤ Options ▾

Names
◆ Default Explode

Properties >>   Close

Figure 21–9

General Steps

Use the following general steps to create a customized exploded view:

1. Enter a name for the explode state.

2. Customize the explode position of the components.

3. Define the offset lines, as needed.

4. Toggle the explode status of the components, as needed.

5. Update the explode state.

Step 1 - Enter a name for the explode state.

Click **New** in the *Explode* area in the View Manager dialog box. Enter a name for the explode and press <Enter>. The new explode is now active, as indicated by ➡.

Step 2 - Customize the explode position of the components.

Click **Properties >>** to define the view properties. The View Manager dialog box opens as shown in Figure 21–10.

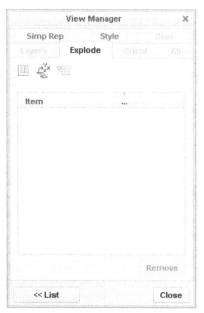

Figure 21–10

Click 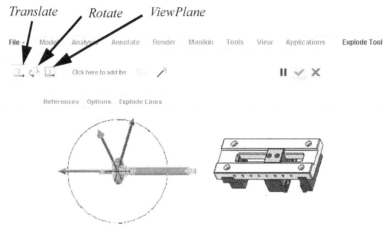 to open the *Explode Position* tab, as shown in Figure 21–11. Use the options in the dialog box to define the component positions or use the arrows in the view window to move the component in the required direction.

Figure 21–11

Use the following steps to modify the position of components:

For example, a planar surface can be selected as the motion reference when repositioning a component in an exploded assembly view. The component is then restricted to move in a direction that is parallel to the planar motion reference.

1. Select the *References* tab to open the Reference panel. Activate the *Movement Reference* area and select an **Axis** or **Straight Edge** as the motion reference.

2. Click ⟶ (Translation), ⟳ (Rotation), or ⟶ (Move normal to a plane) for the type of movement you want. You can also use the arrows in the view window to drag the component.

3. Select the component to move. A arrows display.

4. Use the left mouse button to drag the handle and place the component, as required. The assembly in Figure 21–12 is shown in an exploded view.

Figure 21–12

5. Click  to close the *Explode Tool* tab once all of the components have been moved.

The View Manager dialog box opens as shown in Figure 21–13, displaying a list of exploded components.

Figure 21–13

6. Select a component in the View Manager dialog box and click Remove to unexplode only the selection. Repeat this step, as needed.

Step 3 - Define the offset lines, as needed.

Offset lines enable you to display exploding lines when the assembly is in the explode state. The lines help to explain how the assembly components are assembled to one another.

To create offset lines, click . In the Edit Position tab, click and select two references to define the extent of the line. The references can be an axis, surface normal, or edge/curve. Once created, you can modify, delete, or change the line style for the line.

Step 4 - Toggle the explode status of the components, as needed.

Click ⊙⊞ and ⊞ along the top of the View Manager dialog box to toggle the position of the selected components between the exploded and unexploded states.

Click ⊙⊞ to only unexplode a selected component. Alternatively, you can remove the component from the explode state.

Step 5 - Update the explode state.

Click   << List   to return to the explode listing. The current

explode (indicated by ➥) is temporarily modified with the new settings and displays with a plus (+) symbol appended to the end of its name. For example, A (+) indicates that the A explode was displayed and that it has been changed.

Explode can also be updated by clicking

Edit ▾ *and selecting* **Save**.

To update the changes in the model, right-click and select **Save**. The Save Display Elements dialog box opens as shown in Figure 21–14.

Click   OK   to finish the save action.

Figure 21–14

You can also click

Edit ▾ *and clear the checkmark next to the* **Explode State** *option.*

To unexplode the view, right-click in the View Manager dialog box and select **Explode** to clear the checkmark next to the option or click ⊞ in the Model Display group in the *Model* tab.

21.4 Interference Checks

 Check for interference between the components of the assembly using the Global Interference Analysis command.

Creo Parametric can check for interference between all of the components in your assembly. It reports the parts involved and the volume of interference. This information is used for ensuring that once a model is manufactured, costly interference conflicts do not occur.

General Steps

Use the following general steps to conduct an interference check on an assembly:

1. Access the **Global Interference Analysis** options.

2. Conduct the global interference analysis.

3. Review the results of the global interference analysis.

4. Resolve any conflicts and reanalyze the assembly, as needed.

Step 1 - Access the Global Interference Analysis options.

To conduct a global interference check, click  (Global Interference) in the Inspect Geometry group in the *Analysis* tab. The Global Interference dialog box opens as shown in Figure 21–15.

Figure 21–15

Step 2 - Conduct the global interference analysis.

To conduct the analysis using the default options, click . This performs a global interference check between parts in the assembly. Otherwise, select options in the *Analysis* tab shown in Figure 21–16, to refine the check.

Save options

Figure 21–16

Step 3 - Review the results of the global interference analysis.

Once  has been selected, any interfering parts are identified in the *Results* area in the Global Interference dialog box. In addition, the interfering parts are highlighted in the main window, as shown in Figure 21–17.

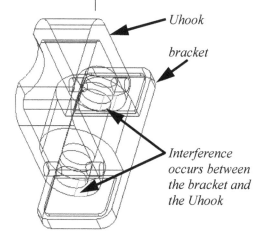

Uhook

bracket

Interference occurs between the bracket and the Uhook

Figure 21–17

Step 4 - Resolve any conflicts and reanalyze the assembly, as needed.

To resolve any interference conflicts, activate one of the components listed in the *Results* area and use the **Edit** or **Edit Definition** options to make the required changes. Once you have modified the components, conduct another global interference check to ensure that all of the conflicts have been resolved.

21.5 Bill of Materials

 Generate a bill of materials for the assembly to determine what components are used and how often.

A Bill of Materials (BOM) can be generated quickly to display a complete list of all of the components in the assembly.

General Steps

Use the following general steps to create a Bill of Materials for an assembly:

1. Access the **Bill of Materials** options.

2. Generate the Bill of Materials report.

3. Investigate the Bill of Materials report.

Step 1 - Access the Bill of Materials options.

To create a Bill of Materials, click (Bill of Materials) in the Investigate group in the *Tools* tab, to open the BOM dialog box, as shown in Figure 21–18.

Figure 21–18

Step 2 - Generate the Bill of Materials report.

Click OK to display the default Bill of Materials for the top-level assembly in the Browser Window, as shown in Figure 21–19.

Step 3 - Investigate the Bill of Materials report.

The Bill of Materials for the U-hook assembly shown at the top of Figure 21–19 displays as shown in Figure 21–19.

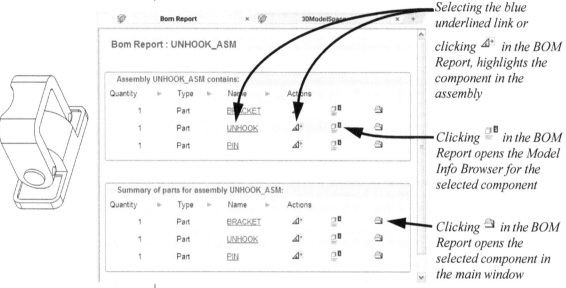

Selecting the blue underlined link or clicking ⬩ in the BOM Report, highlights the component in the assembly

Clicking ▤ in the BOM Report opens the Model Info Browser for the selected component

Clicking ◱ in the BOM Report opens the selected component in the main window

Figure 21–19

Creo Parametric automatically saves the file with a .bom extension (e.g., u_hook.bom.1), containing the BOM in plain text format.

Once the BOM Report displays, you can review it in the Browser window or you can save or print it. To save the report in HTML format, click 💾 at the top of the Browser window. To print the report, click 🖶 at the top of the Browser window.

21.6 Assembly Layers

 Hide, unhide, and isolate layers using the layer tree in an assembly.

The Graphics and Layer dialog boxes in Figure 21–20 show items that were added to layers in the assembly and the display status that was set for the layers.

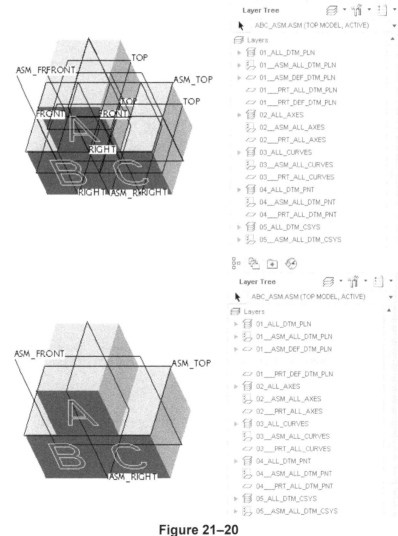

Figure 21–20

Exercise 21a | Datum Plane Assembly

 Locate components in an assembly using the datum planes and axis as constraint references.

 Edit existing components within an assembly using the proper editing tools.

 Check for interference between the components of the assembly using the Global Interference Analysis command.

 Generate a bill of materials for the assembly to determine what components are used and how often.

 Learn how to use the layer tree in an assembly to hide, unhide, and isolate layers.

In this exercise, you will assemble three components to create the assembly shown in Figure 21–21. For clarity, the component datum planes are not shown in this graphic. Once they are assembled, conduct a global interference check, and fix any interferences that are found. Also, activate the handle component and create a feature on it while working in Assembly mode. To complete the exercise, generate the Bill of Materials for the assembly, explode it, and make dimensional changes to the assembly constraints to simulate motion.

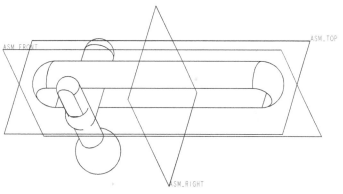

Figure 21–21

Goal | After you complete this exercise, you will be able to:

✓ **Assemble with datum planes**
✓ **Make changes to the assembly and its components**

✓ **Conduct a global interference check**
✓ **Create a Bill of Materials**
✓ **Explode an assembly**

Task 1 - Create a new assembly.

---

1. Change the working directory to the *exercise 21a* folder.

2. Select **File > New** and select **Assembly** in the dialog box to create a new assembly called [slider] using the default template.

3. Ensure that the Datum plane tags are set to show.

Task 2 - Assemble the base component.

Use ✗ in the Component Placement tab to flip the component if the orientation is not correct.

1. Assemble **guide.prt**. Apply a Default constraint.

2. Click ✓. The assembly displays as shown in Figure 21–22.

Figure 21–22

Task 3 - Assemble a part using datum planes.

---

1. Assemble **bar.prt**.

2. Click ▤ ▾ > **Layer tree**. This displays the layer tree.

*You can also scroll down in the layer tree for the assembly, expand the AXIS layer, and unhide **GUIDE.PRT** to show the axis.*

3. Click ▼ in the Layer Tree as shown in Figure 21–23, and select the **bar.prt**. This shows the layers for the **bar.prt**.

Figure 21–23

---

4. Select the **AXIS** layer, right-click, and select **unhide** as shown in Figure 21–24. You can now use the Axis in **bar.prt** to assemble the part.

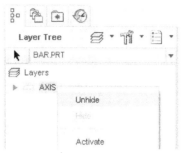

Figure 21–24

5. Click 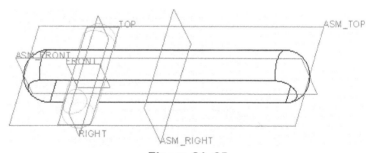 **> Model Tree**.

6. Assign a Distance constraint to datum plane RIGHT of the component with datum plane ASM_RIGHT of the assembly. Enter an offset value of [5]. Use [-5] if you need to flip the new component to the opposite side of datum plane ASM_RIGHT.

7. Assign a Coincident constraint to datum plane TOP of the component to datum plane ASM_TOP of the assembly.

8. Assign a Coincident constraint to datum plane FRONT of the component to datum plane ASM_FRONT on the assembly. The assembly displays as shown in Figure 21–25.

Figure 21–25

9. Click .

Task 4 - Assemble the part called handle.prt.

1. Assemble **handle.prt**.

2. Click ▭ ▾ **> Layer tree**. This displays the layer tree.

3. Click ▾ in the Layer Tree and select the **handle.prt**.

4. Select the **AXIS** layer, right-click, and select **unhide**.

5. Assign a Coincident constraint to axis A_1 of the handle with axis A_4 of the shaft, as shown in Figure 21–26.

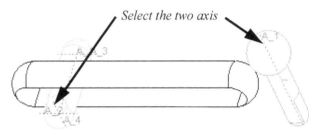

Figure 21–26

6. Assign a Distance constraint to datum plane TOP of the component with datum plane ASM_TOP of the assembly. Enter an offset value of [3]. If necessary, click ✎ in the *Component Placement* tab.

7. Assign a Parallel constraint to the planar surface on the handle with datum plane ASM_FRONT on the assembly, as shown in Figure 21–27.

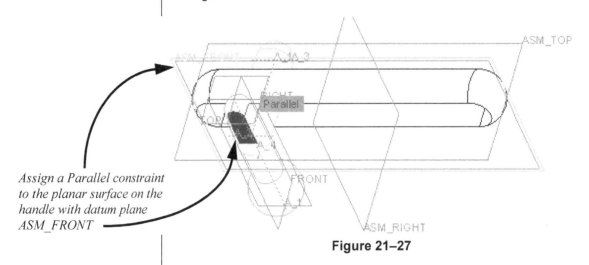

Assign a Parallel constraint to the planar surface on the handle with datum plane ASM_FRONT

Figure 21–27

Task 5 - Perform an interference check on the assembly.

1. Select the *Analysis* tab. Click (Global Interference) in the Inspect Geometry group.

2. Accept the default selections and click . The *Results* area in the dialog box should indicate an interference between the shaft and the handle.

3. Click . The Information window identifies the interfering parts and the volume of interference.

4. Close the Information window and the Global Interference dialog box.

Task 6 - Modify the diameter of the handle.

1. In the Navigator window, click **>Tree Filters**. In the *Display* area in the Model Tree Items dialog box, select the **Features** option to display the assembly and part features in the model tree.

When a component is activated from Assembly mode, displays next to its name.

2. Select the handle component in the model tree.

3. Right-click and select **Activate**.

4. In the model tree, expand **handle.prt**. Select **protrusion id 7** of the handle, right-click, and select **Edit** to display its dimensions.

5. Select the **1.55** diameter dimension and enter [1.49].

6. Click to regenerate the model.

7. In the model tree, select **SLIDER.ASM**, right-click, and select **Activate** to reactivate the assembly.

8. Do another interference check. Are there any other interferences?

Task 7 - Create a round on the handle without leaving Assembly mode.

In this task you will create the round feature shown in Figure 21–28.

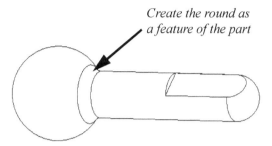

Create the round as a feature of the part

Figure 21–28

1. Select the handle, right-click and select **Activate**.

2. Click to create a constant edge round.

3. Select the edge shown in Figure 21–29.

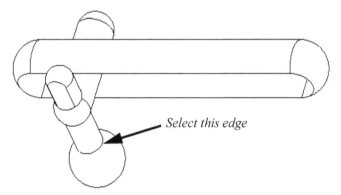

Select this edge

Figure 21–29

4. For the radius of the round, enter [0.5]. Complete the feature.

5. In the model tree, select **SLIDER.ASM**, right-click, and select **Activate** to reactivate the assembly.

6. Open the handle part in Part mode. Although it was created while in Assembly mode, the round is a feature of the handle part, as shown in Figure 21–30.

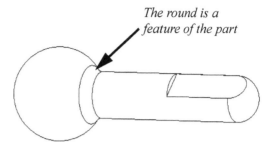

The round is a feature of the part

Figure 21–30

7. Close this window and activate the window containing the assembly.

Task 8 - Create a Bill of Materials.

---

1. Select the *Tools* tab and click ⬚ (Bill of Materials) in the Investigate group.

2. Select the **Top Level** option and click **OK** in the BOM dialog box. The Bill of Materials displays in the Information window.

3. Click ⬚ and save the BOM report as an HTML file.

4. Close the Browser Window.

Task 9 - Simulate motion in the assembly.

An assembly dimension is created when the **Distance Align Offset** constraint is used. In this task you will modify this dimension to simulate motion in the assembly.

1. Double-click on the shaft component in the main window. Select the offset dimension that displays and change it to [0].

2. Click 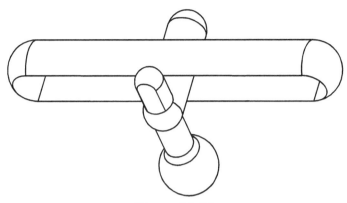 to regenerate the assembly. The assembly displays as shown in Figure 21–31.

Figure 21–31

3. Save the assembly and erase it from memory.

Exercise 21b | Explode Assembly

 Learn to use the View Manager and create an exploded view.

 Learn to move one or multiple components and create snap lines for the exploded view.

In this exercise, you will explode components of the assembly shown in Figure 21–32.

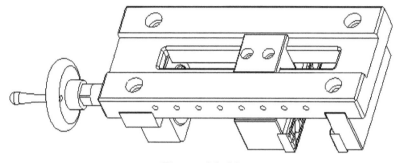

Figure 21–32

Goal

After you complete this exercise, you will be able to:

✓ **Explode an assembly**

Task 1 - Open an assembly file.

1. Set the working directory to the *exercise 21b* folder.

2. Open the assembly called **vise_final.asm.**

Task 2 - Explode the assembly.

You can also click the **View Manager** *icon in the Graphics Toolbar.*

1. Select the *Model* tab and click  (Manage Views) **> View Manager** in the Model Display group. The View Manager dialog box opens as shown in Figure 21–33.

Figure 21–33

2. Select the *Explode* tab, as shown in Figure 21–34.

Figure 21–34

3. In the *Explode* area in the View Manager dialog box, click New . For the explode, enter [explode1] and press <Enter>. The new explode is now active, as indicated by ➡.

4. Click Properties >> to define the view properties.

Task 3 - Modify the position of the components in the exploded view.

---

1. Click ⤳ to define the component positions in the *Explode Tool* tab, as shown in Figure 21–35.

Figure 21–35

2. Select the References slide-up panel. Select **SPINDLE_FINAL_VISE.ASM** in the model tree. Drag the axis to the location shown in Figure 21–36.

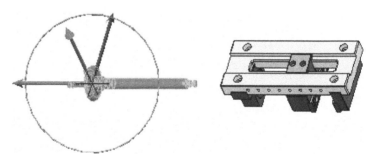

Figure 21–36

Be careful to select a subassembly when it makes sense to do so.

3. Select additional components or subassemblies and experiment with the options to obtain the exploded view shown in Figure 21–37. Select the component to move under the Reference panel and the motion reference. If you make a mistake, correct it using ↺.

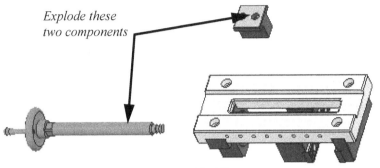

Explode these two components

Figure 21–37

4. Click   References   to activate the *Components to Move* selection area.

5. In the model tree, press <Ctrl> and select the three subassemblies shown in Figure 21–38:

   • **Bearing_Support_Final_Vise.asm**
   • **Support_End_Final_Vise.asm**
   • **Support_Middle_Final_Vise.asm.**

Figure 21–38

You can also select the appropriate Movement Reference in the References panel.

6. Use the left mouse button to drag and place the components, as required. You can select the axis on the drag handle in the direction in which you want the component to move as shown in Figure 21–39.

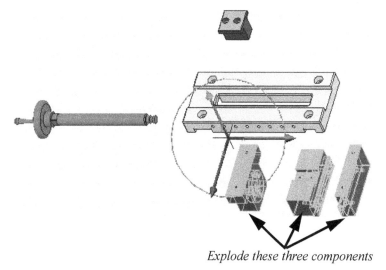

Explode these three components

Figure 21–39

7. If you are not satisfied with the position of the components, you can click ⊞ in the *Explode Position* tab to return the component to its original position.

8. Click ✓ in the *Explode Position* tab. The View Manager dialog box opens as shown in Figure 21–40.

Figure 21–40

9. Click . Click to create explode lines. The Cosmetic Offset Line dialog box opens as shown in Figure 21–41.

Figure 21–41

10. Select the axes to define the explode offset lines and click Apply after each selection. Continue creating explode lines. The assembly displays as shown in Figure 21–42.

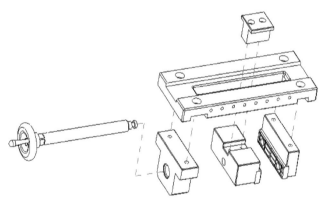

Figure 21–42

11. Click Close . This returns you to the *Explode Tool* tab.

12. Use the Explode Lines panel in the tab to manipulate the existing explode lines. Select a existing explode line and select an option in the Explode Lines panel, as shown in Figure 21–43.

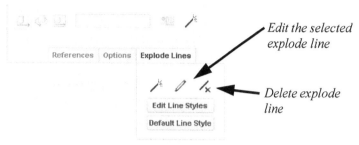

Figure 21–43

13. Click ✓ to return to the listing of the explode. The current explode (indicated by ➔), is temporarily modified with the new settings and displayed with a plus (+) symbol appended to the end of its name. To update the changes in the model, right-click and select **Save**. The Save Display Elements dialog box opens. Click

    OK to finish the **Save** action.

14. Close the View Manager dialog box.

15. Save the assembly and close all of the windows.

16. Erase all the files.

Exercise 21c | Using Layers in Large Assemblies

 Hide, unhide, and isolate layers using the layer tree in an assembly.

 Select components in the assembly using the layer tree.

In this exercise, you will open an existing assembly and use the **Layers** tools to control the display of components in the model. You will also use layers to quickly select components to suppress, resume, and delete.

Goal

After you complete this exercise, you will be able to:

✓ **Use layers to hide and unhide components**
✓ **Use layers as a selection tool**

Task 1 - Open an assembly file.

---

1. Set the working directory to the *exercise 21c* folder.

Ensure that all of the files have been erased from memory before opening this assembly.

2. Open **sorter.asm**. The assembly displays as shown in Figure 21–44.

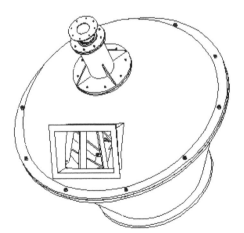

Figure 21–44

Task 2 - Investigate the assembly.

1. Select **casing.asm**, right-click, and select **Open** to open the assembly in a new window. Review the components that exist in this assembly.

2. Click 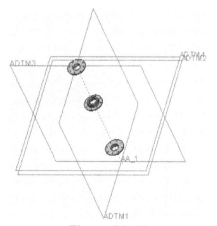 and select **SORTER.ASM** to activate the window.

3. Open the **basket.asm** and **driver.asm** subassemblies in separate windows for further investigation.

4. Close the **casing.asm**, **basket.asm**, and **driver.asm** windows once you are familiar with them.

Task 3 - Hide existing layers.

1. Click and select **SORTER.ASM** to display the top-level assembly.

2. Click and select **Layer Tree** to display the list of model layers.

3. Select the first layer, press <Shift> and select the last layer. All of the layers in the layer tree are selected.

4. Right-click and select **Hide** to hide all of the layers.

5. Click to update the display, if necessary. Only the components shown in Figure 21–45 should be displayed. These components are not included in any layer.

Figure 21–45

6. Click ▤ ▾ and select **Model Tree** to return to the model tree display.

7. The layer status for each component can be displayed in the model tree. Click 🗂 ▾ and select **Tree Columns**. The Model Tree Columns dialog box opens.

8. In the Type drop-down list, select **Layer** as shown in Figure 21–46.

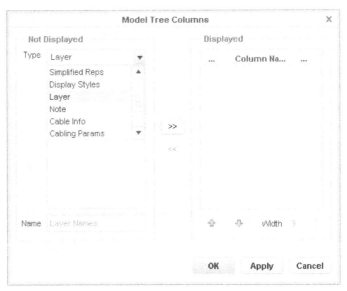

Figure 21–46

9. In the field below the Type drop-down list, select **Layer Status** and click ▸▸ to add Layer Status to the *Displayed* column.

10. Click OK . The model tree displays as shown in Figure 21–47. Flanges are the only displayed components. Expand the list for the patterned components in the top-level assembly. Note that they also have **Hidden** listed as their Layer Status.

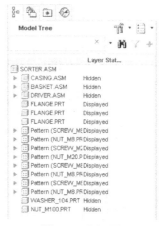

Figure 21–47

Task 4 - Create a new layer.

1. Click and select **Layer Tree** to return to the layer tree display.

2. Right-click and select **New Layer**.

3. For the layer name in the Layer Properties dialog box, type [flanges]. DO NOT press <Enter>.

4. Click > **Model Tree**.

5. In the model tree, select the three **FLANGE.PRT** components. The Layer Properties dialog box opens as shown in Figure 21–48.

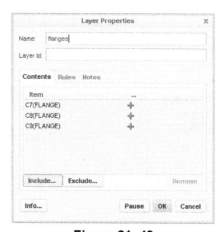

Figure 21–48

6. Click **OK**.

7. Return to the layer tree display and note that this layer is the only one that is not hidden, as indicated by the symbol.

Task 5 - Determine the content of all of the layers.

1. To determine the contents of each layer, select any layer name in the layer tree, right-click, and select **Layer Info**. An Information window opens, displaying the current display status of the layer, as well as a list of all of the items contained on the layer. Close the Information window when you have finished reviewing its content.

*Layer items are highlighted if the **Highlight Geometry** option (accessible through the ▾ flyout) is selected.*

2. To highlight the items that are placed on a layer, select a layer name in the layer tree.

3. Select the **FLANGES** layer in the layers tree.

4. Select the **DRIVER** layer in the layers tree. All components on the layer highlight, even if they are hidden.

Task 6 - Isolate the DRIVER layer.

1. Turn off the display of all datum features using the toolbar icons (e.g., click to turn off the display of datum planes).

2. Select all of the layers in the layer tree, right-click, and select **Unhide**. All of the components are returned to the display.

When a large number of layers exists and you want to display the contents of a single layer, it is faster to Isolate the single layer than to hide all of the others.

3. Select the **DRIVER** layer in the layer tree. Click ▾ and select **Isolate**. Repaint the screen. The assembly displays as shown in Figure 21–49.

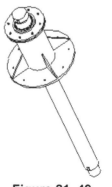

Figure 21–49

4. Create a layer named [test].

5. Click ▶ next to the **DRIVER** layer to expand it. The only item on this layer is the driver assembly.

6. Select the **DRIVER** assembly in the **DRIVER** layer. It is added to the **TEST** layer that you just created.

7. Click **OK** to complete the layer.

8. Hide the **TEST** layer. Why does the model remain unchanged?

9. Right-click on Layers at the top of the layer tree and select **Select Layers** as shown in Figure 21–50. All of the layers are selected.

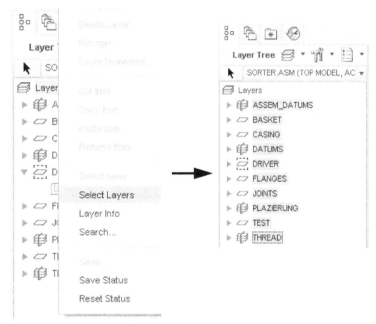

Figure 21–50

10. Right-click on any layer in the tree and select **Unhide**. All of the layers are now visible.

Task 7 - Use layers as a selection tool.

---

1. Suppressing all of the screws and nuts individually can be time-consuming. All of these components are contained on the **JOINTS** layer. Therefore, they can be quickly suppressed by selecting the layer. Select the **JOINTS** layer in the layer tree.

2. All of the components highlight on the screen. However, they are not actually selected. Right-click and select **Select Items**.

3. Return to the model tree display, right-click, and select **Suppress** and confirm the suppression of these components from the model.

4. Note that the model tree updates with the items removed, as shown in Figure 21–51.

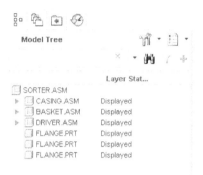

Figure 21–51

Suppressed features and components can be displayed in the model tree by clicking *and selecting **Tree Filters > Suppressed Objects**. Suppressed items have a black square next to their names.*

5. Use the same technique to suppress the **BASKET** layer. Some of the components in this layer have children. Suppress them as well.

6. To resume all suppressed components, select the *Model tab* and select **Operations > Resume > Resume All**.

7. Save the assembly.

8. Close all windows and erase from memory.

Review Questions

1. By default, components that reference datum planes are assembled on the dominant brown side of the datum plane. Which of the following icons do you select to flip a component's orientation direction?

    a.

    b.

    c.

    d.

2. Datum planes can be used as constraint references when defining component placements.

    a. True

    b. False

3. Which of the following statements are true regarding making changes to components while in Assembly mode? (Select all that apply.)

    a. Features cannot be added to a component of an assembly while in Assembly mode.

    b. To make changes to an offset assembly constraint value, you can use the **Edit** option.

    c. To make changes to constraint references, you can use the **Edit** option.

    d. To change a feature dimension associated with a component in an assembly, select the component in the model tree, right-click, and select **Active**.

4. A Bill of Materials report generates a complete list of all of the components in an assembly.

    a. True

    b. False

5. Which of the following model tree icons indicates that an assembly component is active?

   a.

   b.

   c.

   d.

6. Which of the following statements are true regarding exploding assemblies? (Select all that apply.)

   a. To explode an assembly, click (Manage Views) in the *Model* tab, and select the *Explode* tab.

   b. The default explode position for assembly components is based on the constraints that were used to assemble the components.

   c. A planar surface can be selected as the motion reference when repositioning a component in an exploded assembly view.

   d. A straight edge can be selected as a motion reference.

7. Which of the following items are reported in a Global Interference check? (Select all that apply.)

   a. Component names.

   b. Volume of interference.

   c. Interfering material is highlighted in red.

   d. Interfering components are highlighted in the model.

Command Summary

Button	Command	Location
▱	**Datum Plane**	• **Ribbon:** *Model* tab in the *Datum* group
	Manage Views	• **Ribbon:** *Model* tab in the *Model Display* group • **Ribbon:** *View* tab in the *Model Display* group • Graphics toolbar
	Toggle Status	• **Ribbon:** *Model* tab in the *Model Display* group • **Ribbon:** *View* tab in the *Model Display* group
	Exploded View	• **Ribbon:** *Model* tab in the *Model Display* group • **Ribbon:** *View* tab in the *Model Display* group
	Bill of Materials	• **Ribbon:** *Tools* tab in the *Investigate* group
	Global Interference	• **Ribbon:** *Analysis* tab in the *Inspect Geometry* group

Chapter 22

Model Information

Creo Parametric provides you with several tools that can be used to obtain information about a part's measurements and mass properties. Cross-sections can also be created to further analyze a model.

This chapter introduces:

✓**Measure Analysis**

✓**Mass Properties**

✓**Creating Cross-sections**

✓**Drawing Annotations**

✓**Changing Model Units**

Learning Objectives

This chapter provides instruction to enable you to do the following:

22.1 Measure Analysis

 Learn how to efficiently access the measurement tools using the Ribbon.

 Measure the distance between geometry using the **Distance** command.

 Learn how to save or create a feature for the measurement.

22.2 Mass Properties

 Learn how to efficiently access the mass properties tool using the Ribbon.

 Set the type and run the analysis.

22.3 Creating Cross-sections

 Create a cross-section using one of the two methods.

 Create the cross-section using options in the *Section* tab.

 Activate, deactivate, or show the cross-section using the model tree or the View Manager dialog box.

22.4 Drawing Annotations

 Create annotations on a newly created annotation plane or a predefined reference plane.

 Show annotations using the appropriate tools in the *Annotation tab*.

22.5 Changing Model Units

 Set, create, and change the model units using the Model Properties dialog box.

22.1 Measure Analysis

 Learn how to efficiently access the measurement tools using the Ribbon.

 Measure the distance between geometry using the **Distance** command.

 Learn how to save or create a feature for the measurement.

Select the *Analysis* tab to access options to measure specific parameters in your model, as shown in Figure 22–1.

Measure options

Figure 22–1

Use the following general steps to perform a Distance measurement:

1. Select the **Distance Measurement** command.

2. Select the references.

3. Save and determine the Analysis type.

> ## Step 1 - Select the Distance Measurement command.

The process to perform each of the measurement options is similar.

Expand  (Measure) and select **Distance** in the *Analysis* tab to perform a distance analysis. The Distance dialog box opens as shown in Figure 22–2.

Figure 22–2

You can toggle and select a different type of measurement command in the Measure dialog box.

The dialog box can be expanded to display additional options by clicking ▼ as shown in Figure 22–3.

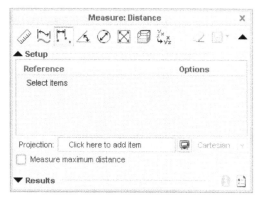

Figure 22–3

Step 2 - Select the references.

Select the required references to measure the distance between the entities. The distance is calculated and displayed in the view window and in the *Results* area in the *Measure dialog box*, as shown in Figure 22–4. The measurement can be expanded or collapsed in the View window.

Use the Measure dialog box to review or change the references, as shown in Figure 22–4.

Click to collapse the measurement display

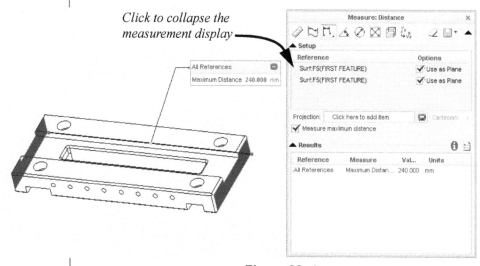

Figure 22–4

Step 3 - Save and determine the Analysis type.

Once the measurement has been created, click  to save, name, or create the measurement as a feature, as shown in Figure 22–5.

Figure 22–5

Table 22–2 describes the types of analysis.

Table 22–1

Type	Description
Saved	The analysis is calculated and the result displayed in the dialog box and graphics window. The definition of the analysis is saved in the model and automatically recalculated when the model changes. To display a saved analysis, click ⌣ in the Manage group in the *Analysis* tab.
Feature	The analysis is calculated and the result displayed in the dialog box. Additionally, an analysis feature is created and shown in the model tree. This option enables you to create feature parameters and datum features based on the analysis.

22.2 Mass Properties

 Learn how to efficiently access the mass properties tool using the Ribbon.

 Set the type and run the analysis.

Select the *Analysis* tab to access options that enable you to run specific analyses on your model as shown in Figure 22–6.

Figure 22–6

The model report options are different in Assembly and Part modes. One of the most common calculations performed is to determine mass properties.

Use the following general steps to perform a quick Mass Properties calculation.

1. Start a Mass Properties calculation.

2. Select the type of analysis.

3. Run the analysis.

Step 1 - Start a Mass Properties calculation.

Click  (Mass Properties) in the *Analysis* tab to calculate the assembly or part mass properties. The Mass Properties dialog box opens as shown in Figure 22–7.

Figure 22–7

Step 2 - Select the type of analysis.

If the model does not have an assigned density, Creo Parametric prompts you to set it before the calculation starts.

By default, the analysis type is set to **Quick**. You can change the type of analysis using the *Analysis* tab. Table 22–2 describes the three types of analysis. In this example, a Quick analysis is performed.

Table 22–2

Type	Description
Quick	The analysis is calculated and the result displayed in the dialog box.
Saved	The analysis is calculated and the result displayed in the dialog box and graphics window. The definition of the analysis is saved in the model and automatically recalculated when the model changes. To access a saved analysis, click ⊞ in the Manage group in the *Analysis* tab.

Type	Description
Feature	The analysis is calculated and the result displayed in the dialog box. Additionally, an analysis feature is created and shown in the model tree. This option enables you to create feature parameters and datum features based on the analysis.

Step 3 - Run the analysis.

Select a coordinate system on the model.

The mass properties of the model are calculated and displayed in the *Results* area in the *Analysis* tab, as shown in Figure 22–8. It is important to note that the calculation does not include information on suppressed features or components.

Figure 22–8

22.3 Creating Cross-sections

 Create a cross-section using one of the two methods.

 Create the cross-section using options in the *Section* tab.

 Activate, deactivate, or show the cross-section using the model tree or the View Manager dialog box.

A cross-section defines a slice through a model as shown in Figure 22–9. Cross-sections can be created in parts and assemblies. Two methods can be used to create cross-sections. The first method requires you to expand ▱ (Section) in the *View* tab and select the type of cross-section you want to create. The second method uses the View Manager dialog box to create a cross-section by selecting the *Section* tab. Table 22–3 describes the types of cross-sections that can be created using either method.

Table 22–3

Option	Description
Planar	A planar cross-section is created using a datum plane in the location of the required slice, as shown on the left in Figure 22–9.
X Direction	A X Direction cross-section is created in the X direction. The location can be changed by entering a value or by dragging the arrow.
Y Direction	A Y Direction cross-section is created in the Y direction. The location can be changed by entering a value or by dragging the arrow.
Z Direction	A Z Direction cross-section is created in the Z direction. The location can be changed by entering a value or by dragging the arrow.
Offset	An offset cross-section is created by sketching a *cut line* to define the required cross-section, as shown on the right in Figure 22–9.
Zone	Zones enable you to divide a component into geometric work regions that can be used to define a condition for rule-driven simplified representations.

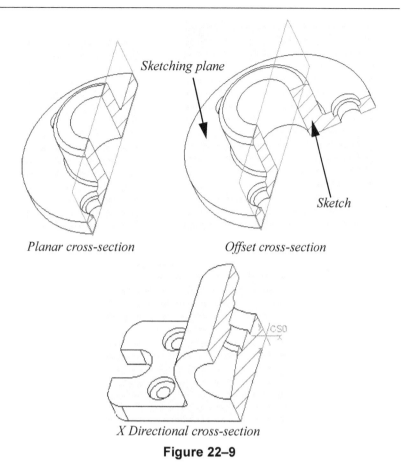

Planar cross-section   *Offset cross-section*

X Directional cross-section

Figure 22–9

Use the following general steps to create a cross-section:

1. Start the creation of a cross-section.

2. Create the cross-section.

3. Select the options for the cross-section.

4. Finalize the cross-section.

5. Modify the cross-hatching.

6. Manage the visibility of the cross-section.

Step 1 - Start the creation of a cross-section.

Method 1

To start the creation of a cross-section, expand  (Section) and select the type of section in the *View* tab, as shown in Figure 22–10.

Figure 22–10

Method 2

You can also click (Manage Views) in the View tab and select the Section tab.

To start the creation of a cross-section, click 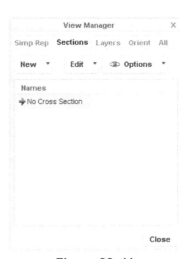 in the graphics toolbar, the View Manager dialog box opens. Select the *Xsec* tab, as shown in Figure 22–11.

The View Manager tabs vary depending on the current mode in which you are working. In Part mode there are four tabs and in Assembly mode there are six.

Figure 22–11

Click [**New** ▾] and select a type of cross-section, as shown in Figure 22–12. Enter a name for the cross-section and press <Enter>.

Figure 22–12

Step 2 - Create the cross-section.

The cross-section definition varies depending on its type.

Planar Cross-section

Select a datum plane or planar surface that defines the location of the cross-section. The Section tab activates as shown in Figure 22–13.

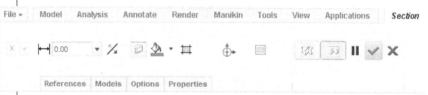

Figure 22–13

You can also change the offset value in the Section tab.

Once the *Section* tab is active, you can dynamically change the offset plane by using the mouse to drag the arrow, as shown in Figure 22–14. You can also turn on the 3D dragger to dynamically translate and rotate the section.

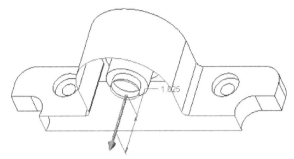

Drag the arrow to change the offset value.

Figure 22–14

Directional Cross-section

The directional cross-section does not require a selection. The location of the cross-section is dependent on the type, default coordinate system, and offset value in the *Section* tab. Once the *Section* tab is active, you can dynamically change the offset plane by using the mouse to drag the arrow, as shown in Figure 22–15. You can also turn on the 3D dragger to dynamically translate and rotate the section.

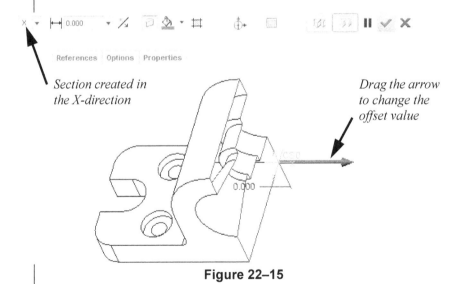

Section created in the X-direction

Drag the arrow to change the offset value

Figure 22–15

Offset Cross-section

The Offset cross-section option enables you to sketch the section using the tools in the *Sketch* tab. The *Section* tab activates once the Offset type has been selected, as shown in Figure 22–16.

Figure 22–16

Select a sketching plane on which you can sketch the cut line for the offset cross-section. In the *Sketch* tab, sketch the required cut line as shown in Figure 22–17.

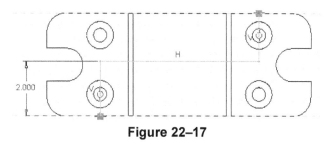

Figure 22–17

Step 3 - Select the options for the cross-section.

Table 22–4 describes the commands and options in the *Section* tab.

Table 22–4

Option	Description
	Flips the clipping direction.
	Caps the surface of the cross-section.
	Opens the section color palette.
	Displays the hatching pattern.
	Toggles on the 3D dragger to dynamically rotate or translate the cross-section.
	Displays a separate window of the 2D view.

Option	Description
	Previews the cross-section without clipping.
	Previews the cross-section with clipping.

You can also dynamically detect any component interference using the Section tool in the Options slide-up panel, as shown in Figure 22–18.

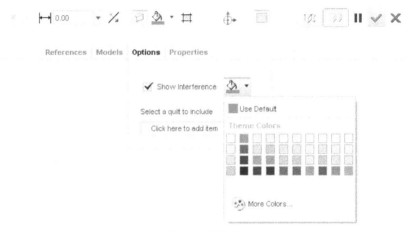

Figure 22–18

Components can be excluded from the section by selecting the Models slide-up panel, as shown in Figure 22–19.

Figure 22–19

Step 4 - Finalize the cross-section.

Click  to complete the cross-section. Cross-sections display in the model tree, as shown in Figure 22–20.

Figure 22–20

Step 5 - Modify the cross-hatching.

When you show the cross-section, it displays with the default line spacing and line angle for the cross-hatching, as shown in Figure 22–21.

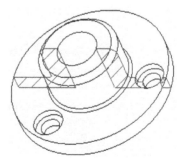

Figure 22–21

You can also expand

Edit ▾ *and select the*
Edit Hatching *option in
the View Manager.*

To modify the default cross-hatching, select the cross-section in the
model tree, right-click, and select **Edit Hatching**. The Edit Hatching
dialog box opens as shown in Figure 22–22.

Figure 22–22

You can select from the hatch library or create your own by setting the
angle and scale values. You can also click ⊿ (Double) or click

⊿ (Half) to change the spacing between the hatching lines. Expand

✎ ▾ to specify the hatching color.

Step 6 - Manage the visibility of the cross-section.

*The tool does not actually
cut the geometry, it is for
visualization purposes
only*

When you finalize the cross-section, it is automatically active and cuts
the model. The active cross-section displays as shown in
Figure 22–23.

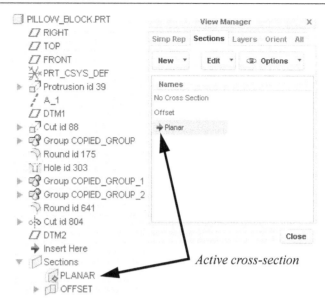

Active cross-section

Figure 22–23

Right-click and select **Deactivate** to disable the cross-section in the model tree or in the View Manager dialog box. You can enable a different cross-section by right-clicking on the section and selecting **Activate**, as shown in Figure 22–24. Only one cross-section can be set as active.

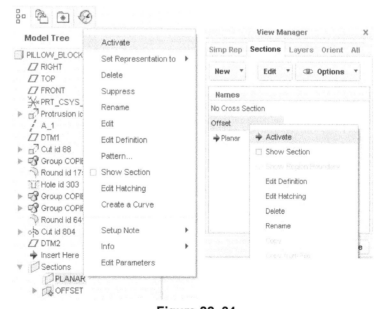

Figure 22–24

You can display the cross-hatching lines, as shown in Figure 22–25, by right-clicking on the section and selecting **Show Section** in the model tree or in the View Manager dialog box. Notice that the symbol in the model tree changes, as shown in Figure 22–25.

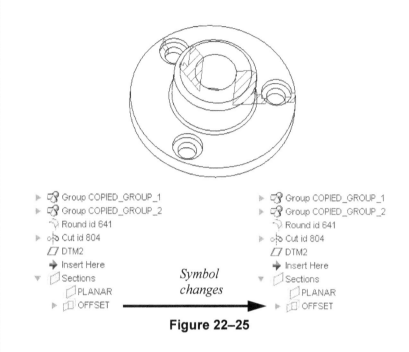

Figure 22–25

22.4 Drawing Annotations

 Create annotations on a newly created annotation plane or a predefined reference plane.

 Show annotations using the appropriate tools in the *Annotation tab*.

Use the following steps to create annotations:

1. Select the *Annotate* tab.

2. Click on a predefined reference plane in the Annotation Planes group, as shown in Figure 22–26.

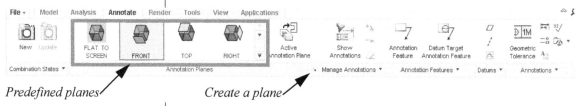

Predefined planes   *Create a plane*

Figure 22–26

You can also create your own annotation plane by clicking ⊠ in the Annotation Planes panel. Click **New** in the Annotation Plane Manager dialog box as show in Figure 22–27.

Figure 22–27

The Active Annotation Orientation dialog box opens as shown in Figure 22–28 and enables you to create your own reference plane.

Figure 22–28

3. Click  (Active Annotation Plane) to set the selected view plane as active.

4. Click (Annotation Feature) in the Annotation Features group in the *Annotate* tab. The Annotation Features dialog box enables you to specify the element that you want to create. The options are shown in Figure 22–29.

Figure 22–29

5. In the Annotation Feature dialog box, click  (Create a Note).

6. In the *Text* area in the Note dialog box, enter [note text] as shown in Figure 22–30.

Figure 22–30

7. Click [Place...] and select a location for the note as shown in Figure 22–31.

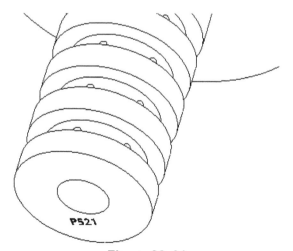

Figure 22–31

Annotation Display

The following two enhancements have been implemented to affect the display of annotation objects:

- To toggle the display of all 3D annotations on and off, click ⬚.
- You can also place annotations so that they always remain parallel (flat-to-screen) to your viewing direction, regardless of how the model is rotated. To set this option, select the *Annotation* tab and click ⬚ in the Annotation Planes group. Select a plane, click

    Edit , and select the **Flat to Screen** option. The **Flat to Screen** options include **Screen Location** and **Geometry Location**. Screen location is independent of geometry, where the annotation height is controlled by the screen units. The **Geometry Location** option permits the annotation to move with the model while remaining flat to the screen and uses model or screen units, as required.

Show Dimensions

Use the following steps to show dimensions.

1. In the model tree, select a feature, right-click, and select **Show Annotations**, as shown in Figure 22–32.

You can also click ⬚ (Show Annotations) in the Manage Annotations group.

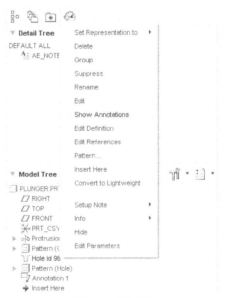

Figure 22–32

The dimensions for the selected feature displays on the active reference plane and the Show Annotations dialog opens as shown in Figure 22–33.

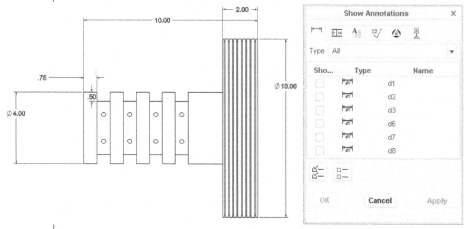

Figure 22–33

2. Select the dimensions you want to keep and click ____OK____ .

Model Tree Settings

3. Click 📋 ˅ and select **Tree Filters**. Select the **Annotations** option as shown in Figure 22–34.

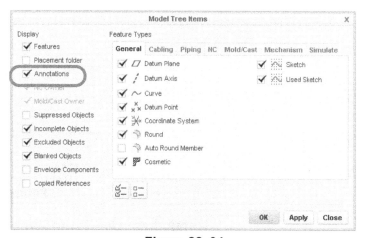

Figure 22–34

4. Click ____OK____ .

5. The note is displayed in the Detail tree and the Model tree. Expand the features in the model tree to display the dimension note.

6. Select **DRV_DIM**, right-click, and select **Move**, as shown in Figure 22–35.

Figure 22–35

7. Select a location for the 3D dimension as shown in Figure 22–36.

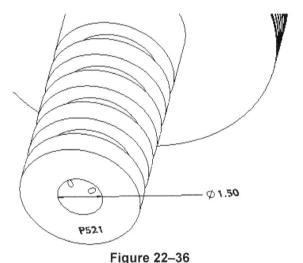

Figure 22–36

Retain Last Used Annotation

When you create an annotation and define the plane, text direction, and viewing angle, the settings are captured and reused for each subsequent annotation until you define new references.

Create Dimensions

You can create dimensions by clicking ⊬⊣ and using the same selection techniques used in drawing mode.

Ordinate Dimensions

You can create ordinate dimensions and baselines within an Annotation feature, as shown in Figure 22–37.

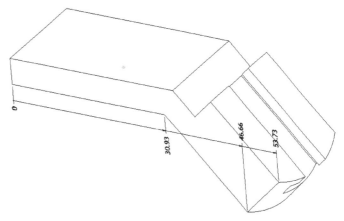

Figure 22–37

Surface Finish

The configuration option (default_placement_surface_finish) is available to customize the default option that is used when placing a surface finish using the Surface Finish dialog box. The default value is **Normal to Entity**; other values include **with Leaders**, **on Entity**, and **Free**.

Surface Profile GTOL

You can create a surface profile geometric tolerance (GTOL) in accordance with the Y14.41 standard. This enables an unequal disposition of the tolerance zone.

22.5 Changing Model Units

 Set, create, and change the model units using the Model Properties dialog box.

Occasionally, the part units in your models might need to be modified. When modifying the part units, you can convert the existing units to the new system of units or you can maintain the current values in the new system.

Use the following general steps to change part units:

1. Start the change of units.

2. Define the new system of units.

3. Define the conversion method.

Step 1 - Start the change of units.

To change the units of your model, select **File > Prepare > Model Properties** to open the Model Properties dialog box as shown in Figure 22–38.

Figure 22–38

Select **Change beside Units** in the *Materials* area in the dialog box. The Units Manager dialog box opens as shown in Figure 22–39.

Figure 22–39

Step 2 - Define the new system of units.

To define a new system of units, you can select from the list of predefined systems or create a new one. A description of the predefined units is listed at the bottom of the Units Manager dialog box. To create a new system of units, click New... . The System of Units Definition dialog box opens as shown in Figure 22–40.

Figure 22–40

To define the new system of units, assign a name and type, and select the required type of units. Click OK to complete the definition.

Step 3 - Define the conversion method.

Select the new system of units and click → Set... to finalize the change of units. The Changing Model Units dialog box opens as shown in Figure 22–41.

Figure 22–41

In the *Model* tab, select how the current dimension values are going to change in the model. You must select one of the following:

- The **Convert Dimensions** option converts the existing dimensions to the new system of units, while maintaining the same size in the resulting model (i.e., 1" becomes 25.4 mm).
- The **Interpret Dimensions** option keeps the same numeric values in dimensions when changing the system of units (i.e., 1" becomes 1 mm).

In the *Parameters* tab, select how the parameters change in the model, as shown in Figure 22–42. The *Parameters* tab lists Real number parameters that only have units assigned to them.

*The **Interpret Dimensions** option can be useful if you accidentally design the model using the wrong units.*

Figure 22–42

Click OK to complete the change of units and close the Units Manager dialog box.

Exercise 22a | Cross-Sections

 Create a planar cross-section using the Section command.

 Create an offset cross-section using the Section command.

In this exercise, you will use the View Manager dialog box to create two types of cross-sections, as shown Figure 22–43.

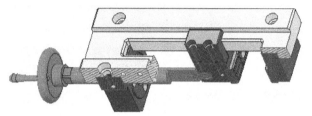

Figure 22–43

Goal

After you complete this exercise, you will be able to:

✓ **Create a planar cross-section**
✓ **Create an offset (sketched) cross-section**

Task 1 - Open an assembly file.

1. Set the working directory to the *exercise 22a* folder.

2. Open **vise_final.asm**.

3. If they are not already displayed, turn on the display of the datum axes and their tags.

4. Show features in the model tree by clicking 🔧 ▼ and selecting **Tree Filters**.

Task 2 - Create an assembly datum plane.

Select the Model tab to create a datum plane.

1. Create an assembly datum plane through the two axes, as shown in Figure 22–44. Rename the plane as [CROSS_SECTION_B].

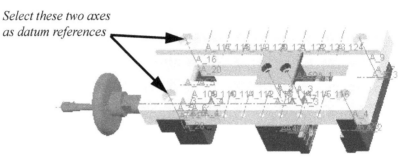

Select these two axes as datum references

Figure 22–44

Task 3 - Create a planar cross-section.

You can also select the View tab to create a section.

1. Select the *Model* tab. Expand ▱ (Section) and select **Planar**. The *Section* tab activates as shown in Figure 22–45.

Figure 22–45

2. Select the Properties slide-up panel and enter [B] for the name.

3. Select the datum plane that you previously created.

4. Complete the cross-section.

5. If necessary, right-click on section B and select **Activate**. The cross-section displays as shown in Figure 22–46. One side of the cross-section is removed from the display.

Figure 22–46

6. In the model tree, right-click on section B and select **Show Section** to display the cross-hatching for the section. The section displays as shown in Figure 22–47.

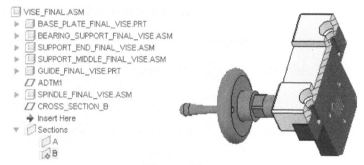

Figure 22–47

7. Turn off cross-hatching for the section

8. Right-click on the section and select **Deactivate** to return the display to normal.

Task 4 - Create an offset cross-section.

1. Expand (Section) and select **Offset** in the *View* tab. The *Section* tab activates.

2. Name the cross-section [C].

3. The message window prompts you to select a sketching plane.

---

4. Select the top-most surface of the assembly as a sketching plane as shown in Figure 22–48.

Select this surface for the sketch plane

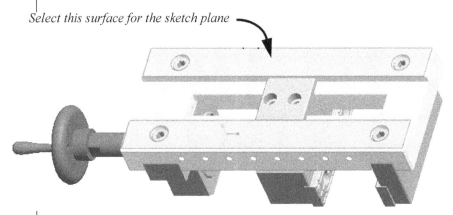

Figure 22–48

5. Once in the *Sketch* tab is active, you need to select the sketching references. Select the left and right sides of **base_plate_final_vise.prt**. Two vertical dashed lines display. Do not close the Reference dialog box.

6. Change the selection filter to **Axis** and select one of the axes shown in Figure 22–49. Change the selection filter to **Axis** again and select the other axis.

Select these axes

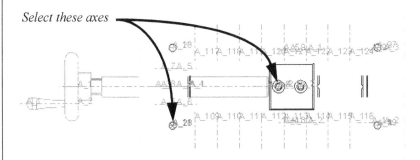

Figure 22–49

7. Close the References dialog box.

8. Create the sketch shown in Figure 22–50.

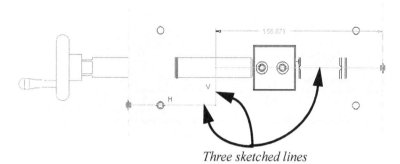

Three sketched lines

Figure 22–50

9. Complete the sketch. The cross-section is complete.

10. Right-click and select **Show Section** to display the cross-hatching for the section. The model should look similar to one shown in Figure 22–51.

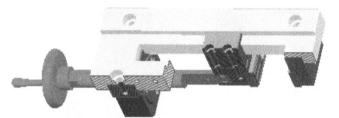

Figure 22–51

11. Save the assembly and erase it from memory.

Exercise 22b | Model Measurements I

 Find the length, height, angle, and the distance between entities using the measurement tools.

In this exercise, you will use the measurement tools to investigate a model. You will use the measurement tools to verify the distance, area, angle, and diameter of various features in the model.

Goal | After you complete this exercise, you will be able to:

✓ **Take specific measurements from a model**

Task 1 - Open a part file.

1. Set the working directory to the *exercise 22b* folder.

2. Open **pillow_block.prt** in the *exercise 3c* folder. The model displays as shown in Figure 22–52.

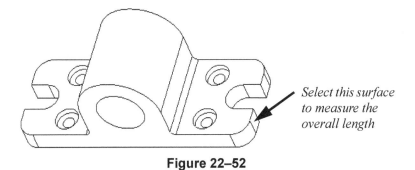

Select this surface to measure the overall length

Figure 22–52

Task 2 - Measure the overall length.

1. Select the *Analysis* tab and click (Measure) > **Distance**.

2. Click ▼ to expand the Measure: Distance dialog box as shown in Figure 22–53.

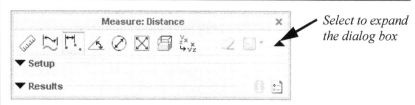

Figure 22–53

3. Click ▼ next to *Setup* and *Results* to expand the Measure dialog box as shown in Figure 22–54.

Figure 22–54

4. Select the vertical planar surface on the right side of the model, as shown in Figure 22–55.

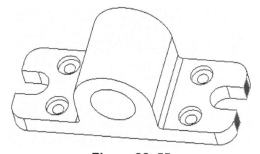

Figure 22–55

5. Hold down <Ctrl> and select a similar vertical planar surface on the left side of the model.

6. The information displayed in the Graphics window and in the Distance dialog box indicates that the distance = 10 as shown in Figure 22–56.

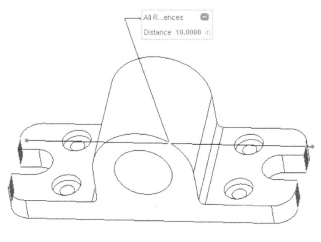

Figure 22–56

7. Do not close the Distance dialog box.

Task 3 - Measure the overall height.

---

*You can also right-click and select **Clear** to clear the selected references or to select new references.*

1. Click in the Measure dialog box to clear the selected references.

2. Select the bottom surface of the part as shown in Figure 22–57.

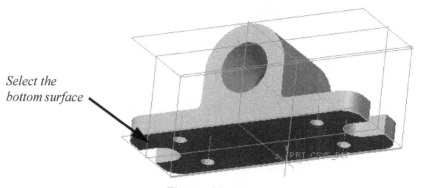

Select the bottom surface ←

Figure 22–57

3. Hold down <Ctrl> and select **DTM2** to measure the overall height as shown in Figure 22–58.

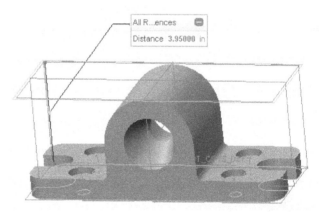

Figure 22–58

4. The information displayed in the Graphics window and in the Distance dialog box indicates that the distance = 3.95.

5. Do not close the Distance dialog box.

Task 4 - Measure a distance between the U-shaped cut and the hole.

---

1. Click ✎ in the Measure dialog box to clear the selected references.

2. Select the cylindrical surface of the U-shaped cut, as shown in Figure 22–59.

3. Hold down <Ctrl> and select the cylindrical surface of the hole, as shown in Figure 22–59.

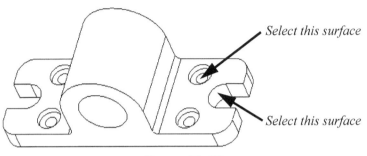

Select this surface

Select this surface

Figure 22–59

4. The information displayed in the Graphics window and in the Distance dialog box indicates that the distance = 1.65.

5. Clear **Use As Axis** for both references in the *References* area of the dialog box. The information displayed in the Graphics window and in the Distance dialog box indicates that the distance = 0.8.

Task 5 - Measure the length of an edge.

*You can also right-click and select **Measure > Length**.*

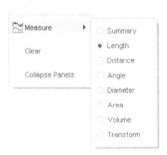

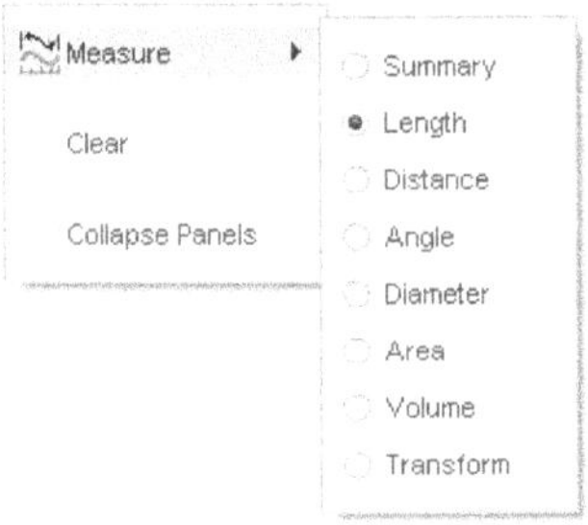

1. Click in the Measure dialog box to clear the selected references.

2. Click in the dialog box.

3. Select the edge as shown in Figure 22–60.

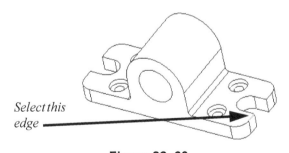

Select this edge

Figure 22–60

4. Right-click in the References collector and select **Use as Chain** as shown in Figure 22–61.

Figure 22–61

5. Select **Rule-based** and ensure that **Tangent** is selected. All of the tangent edges are selected as shown in Figure 22–62.

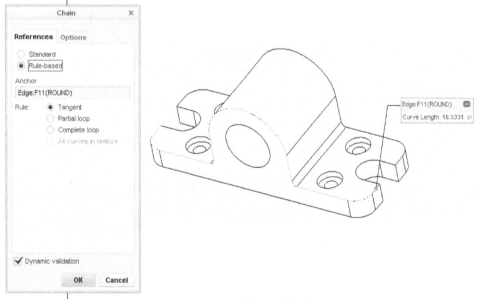

Figure 22–62

6. The information displayed in the Graphics window and in the Length dialog box indicates that the length = 16.53.

Task 6 - Measure point to point with a distance measurement.

1. Click ⟍ in the Measure dialog box to clear the selected references.

2. Click ⊡ᐧ in the Measure dialog box.

3. Select the vertex shown in Figure 22–63.

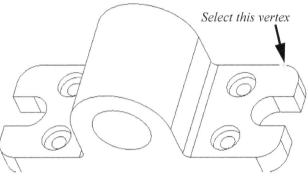

Select this vertex

Figure 22–63

4. Hold down <Ctrl> and select the cylindrical edge shown in Figure 22–64. The centerpoint of the arc is selected by default.

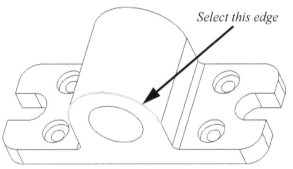

Select this edge

Figure 22–64

5. Select the **Projection** reference collector in the Measure: Distance dialog box as shown in Figure 22–65.

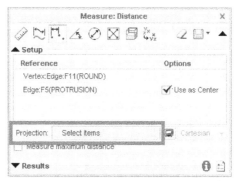

Figure 22–65

6. Select the **PRT_CSYS_DEF** coordinate system. This projects the measurement to the coordinate system. The measurement displays as shown in Figure 22–66.

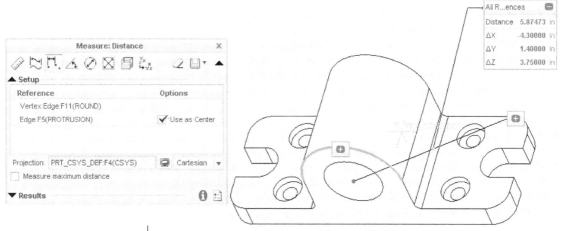

Figure 22–66

Task 7 - Measure an angle between surfaces.

---

1. Click ✐ in the Measure dialog box to clear the selected references.

*You can also right-click and select **Angle**.*

2. Click ⟁ in the Measure dialog box.

3. Select two planar surfaces, as shown in Figure 22–67.

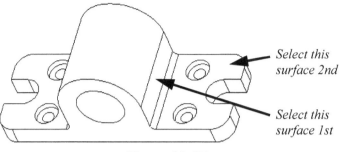

Select this surface 2nd

Select this surface 1st

Figure 22–67

4. The information displayed in the Graphics window and in the Angle dialog box indicates that the angle = 89.

5. Click ˇ and select **Supplement** in the *Angle* field as shown in Figure 22–68. This changes the angle direction with an angle of 91 degrees.

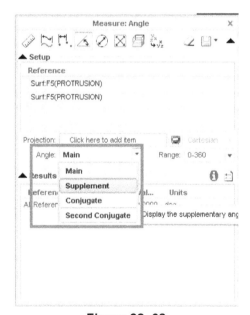

Figure 22–68

6. The information displayed in the Graphics window and in the Angle dialog box indicates that the angle = 91, as shown in Figure 22–69. This is the correct value.

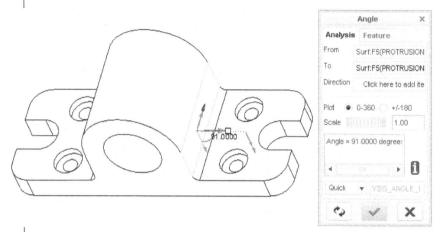

Figure 22–69

Task 8 - Measure the area of a surface.

1. Click ✐ in the Measure dialog box to clear the selected references.

2. Click ⊠ in the Measure dialog box.

3. Select a planar surface as shown in Figure 22–70.

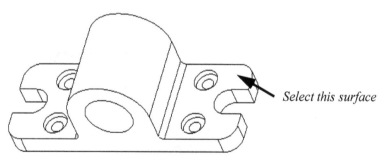

Select this surface

Figure 22–70

4. The information displayed in the Graphics window and in the Area dialog box indicates that the area = 8.11.

Task 9 - Measure the diameter of a surface.

1. Click ∠ in the Measure dialog box to clear the selected references.

2. Click ⊘ in the Measure dialog box.

3. Select a cylindrical surface as shown in Figure 22–71.

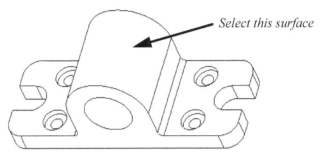

Select this surface

Figure 22–71

4. The information displayed in the Graphics window and in the Diameter dialog box indicates that the diameter = 3.5.

5. Click ✎ in the Measure dialog box. Note that the summary displays the area, perimeter, and diameter.

6. Click 💾 ▾ and select **Save Analysis**.

7. Click **OK** .

8. Close the Measure dialog box.

You can also collapse the measurement in the View window by clicking ⊖ next to the measurement.

9. Click 📊 (Saved Analysis) in the *Analysis* tab.

10. Click **All** ▾ and select **Hide All** to remove the analysis from the View window.

11. Close the Saved Analysis dialog box.

12. Erase the model from memory.

Exercise 22c | 3D Annotations

 Create and activate annotation planes.

 Create and locate new annotation notes on the active plane.

 Show annotations using the appropriate tools in the *Annotation tab*.

In this exercise, you will add 3D annotations to a part. You will add a part number using a note and then show 3D annotation elements. You will set up various reference planes for the annotations. The completed part displays as shown in Figure 22–72.

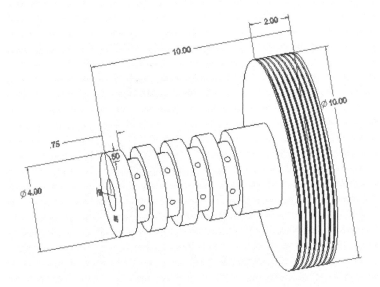

Figure 22–72

Goal | After you complete this exercise, you will be able to:

✓ **Create a 3D note**
✓ **Show dimension annotations**
✓ **Manipulate 3D annotations**

Task 1 - Open a part file.

1. Set the working directory to the *exercise 22c* folder.

2. Open **plunger.prt**. The part displays as shown in Figure 22–73.

Figure 22–73

Task 2 - Set the annotation orientation.

In this task, you will define a surface of the part as the reference plane. This makes it easier to place the part number annotation.

1. Select the *Annotate* tab. Click ⌐ in the Annotation Planes panel as shown in Figure 22–74.

Select the Annotation Planes panel

Figure 22–74

2. The Annotation Plane Manager dialog box opens as shown in Figure 22–75.

Figure 22–75

3. Click New in the Annotation Plane Manager dialog box. The Annotation Plane Definition dialog box opens as shown in Figure 22–76.

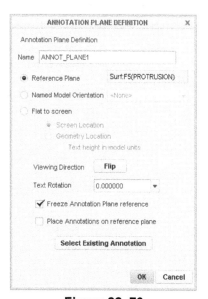

Figure 22–76

4. Select the **Reference Plane** option and select the surface shown in Figure 22–77.

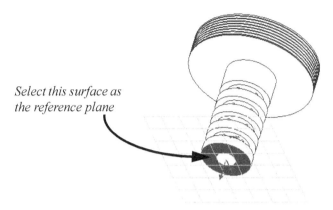

Select this surface as the reference plane

Figure 22–77

Task 3 - Set the viewing direction and text rotation.

1. Click ^{Flip}. In the Text Rotation drop-down list, select **270** as shown in Figure 22–78.

Figure 22–78

The blue arrow indicates the direction for viewing the annotation and the red arrow indicates the direction of the text. Ensure that the arrows display as shown in Figure 22–79.

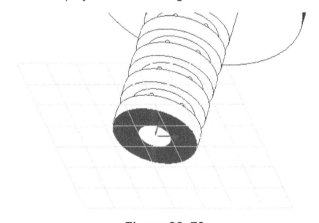

Figure 22–79

2. Click   OK   and close the Annotation Plane Manager.

3. Notice the new annotation plane is selected and added to the
   Annotate tab. Click 🔄 (Active Annotation Plane) to orient the
   model normal to the new plane.

4. Close the Annotation Plane Manager dialog box.

Task 4 - Create an annotation feature.

---

1. Click 🗇 (Annotation Feature) in the *Annotate* tab.

2. Click ⩙ in the Annotation Feature dialog box, as shown in
   Figure 22–80.

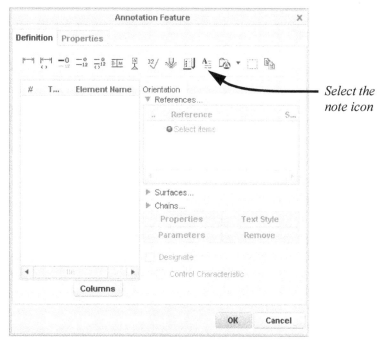

Figure 22–80

3. In the *Text* area in the Note dialog box, for the part number, enter [P521], as shown in Figure 22–81.

Note	×
Name	
Note_0	ID: 0
Parent	
Part	
➤ PLUNGER	
Text	
P521|	

| **Insert** ▼ | Style... | **Symbols...** |

Placement

| **Place...** | Move Text... |
| Mod Attach... | Move... |

URL

Hyperlink...

| **OK** | **Cancel** |

Figure 22–81

4. Click <u>Place...</u>.

5. In the Menu Manager, select **No Leader > Standard > Done**.

6. Select the part number location shown in Figure 22–82.

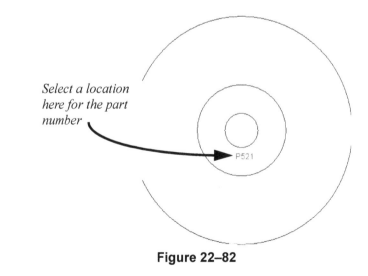

Select a location here for the part number

P521

Figure 22–82

7. In the Note dialog box, click 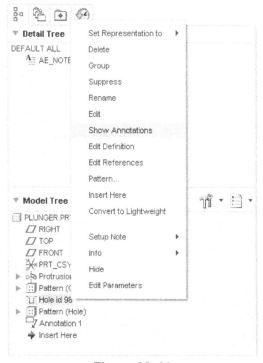 OK and in the Annotation Feature dialog box, click OK .

Task 5 - Show a dimension annotation element.

In this task, you will show an annotation of a feature dimension. The dimension annotation displays on the same plane as the note you created in the last task because that reference plane is still active.

1. In the model tree, select **Hole id 98**, right-click, and select **Show Annotations**, as shown in Figure 22–83.

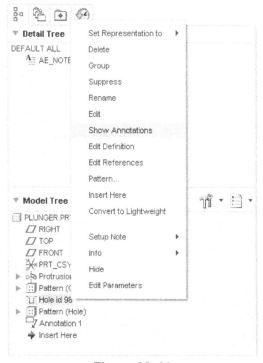

Figure 22–83

2. Select the **d4** dimension as shown in Figure 22–84.

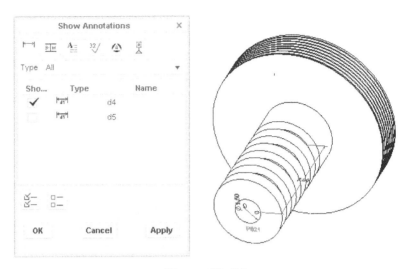

Figure 22–84

3. Click ^{OK} in the Show Annotations dialog box. The dimension displays as shown in Figure 22–85.

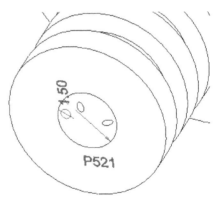

Figure 22–85

Task 6 - Display annotations in the model tree.

In this task, you will move the dimension annotation.

1. Click 📅 ⁻ and select **Tree Filters**. Select the **Annotations** option as shown in Figure 22–86.

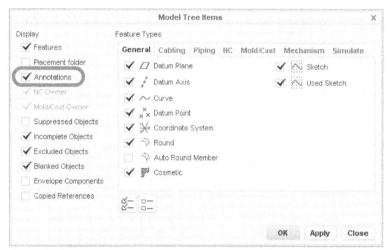

Figure 22–86

2. Click OK .

3. In the model tree, expand **Hole id 98** to display the driving dimension note.

4. Select **DRV_DIM_D4**, right-click, and select **Current Orientation** as shown in Figure 22–87.

Figure 22–87

5. In the *Text Rotation* area in the Annotation Plane dialog box, select **270** in the drop down list. Click **OK** .

6. Select **DRV_DIM_D4** in the view window and drag the dimension to the right of the hole, as shown in Figure 22–88.

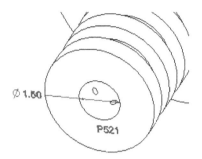

Figure 22–88

Task 7 - Change the active annotation orientation plane.

---

1. The active annotation plane needs to be changed. Select the arrow in the scroll bar next in the Annotation Plane group as shown in Figure 22–89.

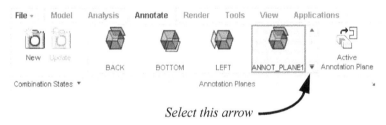

Select this arrow

Figure 22–89

2. Click (Right) in the Annotation Planes group in the *Annotation* tab, as shown in Figure 22–90.

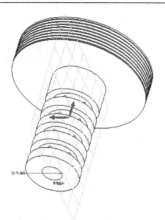

Figure 22–90

3. Click (Active Annotation Plane) in the *Annotate* tab.

4. Right-click on the revolved protrusion (Protrusion id 39) in the model tree, and select **Show Annotations**. The dimensions display on the active reference plane. Select all the dimensions and close the dialog box.

5. Move the dimensions as shown in Figure 22–91.

You can set the filter to

Annotation ▼ *and*
use the contextual menu
options to manipulate the
3D annotations.

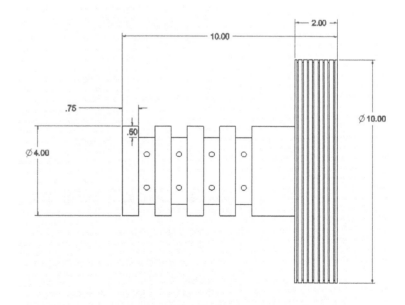

Figure 22–91

6. Save the part and erase it from memory.

Exercise 22d	# Measurements & Annotations (Optional)

 Compare dimensions in the model using the measurement tools in the *Analysis tab*.

 Show and create 3D annotations using the annotation tools.

In this exercise, you will practice taking a variety of measurements and create and show 3D annotations with little instruction.

Goal After you complete this exercise, you will be able to:

✓ **Take specific measurements from a model**
✓ **Create and show 3D annotations**

Task 1 - Open a part file.

---

1. Set the working directory to the *exercise 22d* folder.

2. Open **crank_shaft.prt**. The model displays as shown in Figure 22–92.

Figure 22–92

Task 2 - Take a variety of measurements.

---

1. Select the *Analysis* tab and use the icons in the Measure group to take the measurements shown in Figure 22–93. Descriptions of the types of measurements are listed in Table 22–5. Compare your results to those listed in the table to ensure that the measurements have been taken correctly.

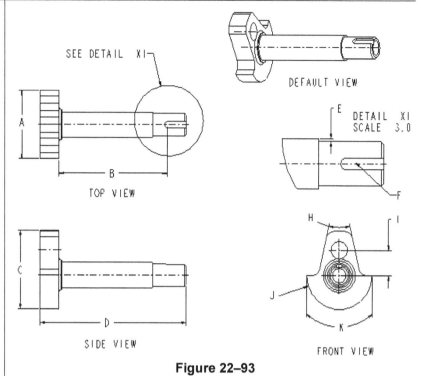

Figure 22–93

Table 22–5

Dimension	Description	Value
A	Overall width of model.	46.00
B	From face to center of arc on slot.	75.00
C	Overall height of model.	53.00
D	Overall length of model.	101.00
E	Height of step.	1.00
F	Surface area of slot.	58.28
H	Angle.	25.46
I	Center to center between shaft and hole.	17.00
J	Diameter.	46.00
K	Arc length.	72.26

Task 3 - Create or show the 3D annotation features.

1. Create or show the 3D annotations shown in Figure 22–94, Figure 22–95, and Figure 22–96.

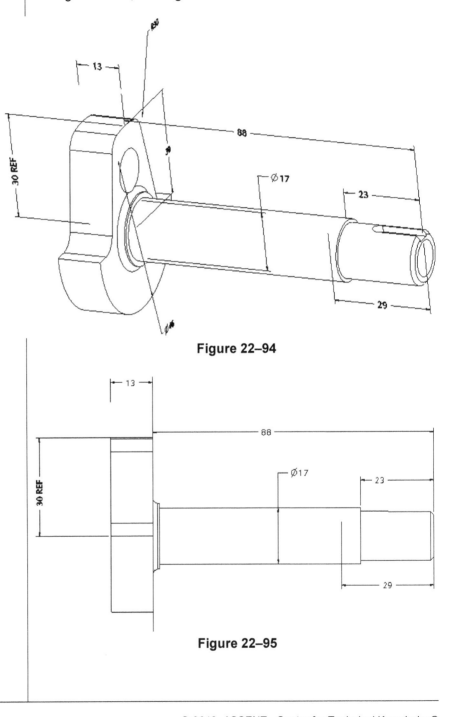

Figure 22–94

Figure 22–95

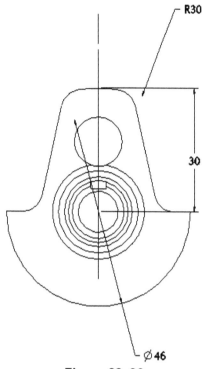

Figure 22–96

2. Save the part and erase it from memory.

Review Questions

1. Analysis tools are only available in Assembly Mode.

   a. True

   b. False

2. Which of the following options saves your analysis in the model?

   a. Quick

   b. Saved

   c. Feature

   d. You cannot save an analysis

3. Which icon enables you to view a distance measurement using the saved option?

   a.

   b.

   c.

   d.

4. Mass Property calculations include information on suppressed features or components.

   a. True

   b. False

5. A _____ cross-section is created using a datum plane in the location of the required slice.

   a. Offset Cross-section

   b. Planar Cross-section

   c. Directional Cross-section

6. Cross-sections physically cut the model.

   a. True

   b. False

7. The _____ option changes existing dimensions to the new system of units (i.e., 1" becomes 25.4 mm).

   a. Convert

   b. Interpret

8. If a model has been created using the wrong units, what is the best conversion method to use?

   a. Convert Dimensions

   b. Interpret Dimensions

   c. You must scale the model

Command Summary

Button	Command	Location
	Measure	• **Ribbon:** *Analysis* tab in the *Measure* group
	Manage Views	• **Ribbon:** *Model* tab in the *Model Display* group • **Ribbon:** *View* tab in the *Model Display* group • Graphics toolbar
	Mass Properties	• **Ribbon:** *Analysis* tab in the *Model Report* group
	Save Analysis	• **Ribbon:** *Analysis* tab in the *Manage* group
	Section	• **Ribbon:** *View* tab in the *Model Display* group • **Ribbon:** *Model* tab in the *Model Display* group
	Annotation Feature	• **Ribbon:** *Annotate* tab in the *Annotation Features* group
	Annotation Display	• Graphics toolbar
	Show Annotations	• **Ribbon:** *Annotate* tab in the *Manage Annotations* group
	Dimension	• **Ribbon:** *Annotate* tab in the *Annotations* group

Chapter 23

Effective Modeling

Before creating any model (part or assembly) in Creo Parametric, you should consider its design intent. Planning ahead helps you select the most appropriate options to maximize design flexibility. This chapter discusses methods that you can use to ensure that you create a model that meets your design goals.

This chapter introduces:

- ✓Design Considerations
- ✓Modeling Tips and Techniques
- ✓Model Investigation
- ✓Interactive Exercise

Learning Objectives

This chapter provides instruction to enable you to do the following:

23.1 Design Considerations

 Learn to ask questions when creating a part or assembly to create a flexible model that communicates the design intent.

23.2 Modeling Tips and Techniques

 Create a flexible model that communicates the design intent using the model tips and best practices.

23.3 Model Investigation

 Modify an existing model using the investigation tools.

23.4 Interactive Exercise

 Create a flexible model that communicates the design intent.

23.1 Design Considerations

 Learn to ask certain questions when creating a part or assembly to create a flexible model that communicates the design intent.

A designer strives to create models that meet the following criteria:

- Communicates design intent.
- Can be manufactured to generate a component that meets the design intent.
- Is flexible so that future design changes require minimal effort.
- Can be used to generate design documentation (i.e., drawings).

Considering *what if* scenarios that can be introduced into the model in the future helps you to create a robust model that requires minimal effort when the time comes for modifications.

Part Design Considerations

Consider the following questions:

- What is the best choice for the base feature?
- Which parent/child relationships are required?
- Which parent/child relationships should be avoided?
- Which dimensions are required to drive the design?
- Which dimensions on the part can change?
- How should the part react to dimension changes?
- Which dimensions are required in the drawing?
- Should relations be added to capture the design intent?
- What feature order best captures the design intent?

Assembly Design Considerations

Consider the following questions:

- What is the best selection for the base component?
- Which assembly constraints capture the design intent?
- Which parent/child relationships are required?
- Which parent/child relationships should be avoided?
- Should a Coincident or Distance constraint be used?
- Is motion to be simulated in the design?
- Should subassembly components be incorporated into the design?
- Should assembly relations be added to capture the design intent?
- What component order best captures the design intent?

23.2 Modeling Tips and Techniques

 Create a flexible model that communicates the design intent using the model tips and best practices.

Many companies have their own design requirements or best practice recommendations. Some of these recommendations include the following:

Features

Features either add or remove material from the model to create the final design. Consider the following tips when adding features to the model:

- Start models with default datum planes.
- Select a stable base feature that does not require many changes. The base feature is used as a parent for additional features.
- Use the feature forms (extrude, revolve, sweep, or blend), feature types (pick and place or sketched), and feature attributes that best capture the design intent.
- Select the references that properly reflect the design intent. Any reference selected while creating a new feature establishes a dependency between them. This is true when you are defining the sketching plane, orientation plane, sketching references, and dimensioning references.
- Use the sketching tools that best capture the design intent.
- Use depth options (**Thru Next**, **Thru Until**, **Thru All**, etc.) to capture the design intent.
- Create features in an order that best captures the design intent.
- Name features so that they can be easily identified in the model tree.

Drafts and Rounds

Review your company standards when considering whether to add drafts to accurately represent your model. For instance, some companies prefer not to add drafts to models, while others insist on it. Some considerations include the following:

- Does adding drafts increase model accuracy or is it going to adversely affect drawing creation?
- If drafts are not added to the model, how do you communicate this requirement to the manufacturer?

- Does the model need to undergo interference or analysis testing? If so, you can add the draft to ensure accurate results.

Rounds generally represent the finishing stages of the design. Similar to drafts, always consider your company standards when deciding whether to add rounds to the model. Some considerations include the following:

- Is the model going to be used for FEA analysis? If so, rounds are generally removed before the analysis and are not required.
- Depending on the type of rounds that make up the model, the manufacturing department can remove rounds that are created at the end of the process. In this situation, you can add all of the rounds and only suppress the ones that are not needed for generating the NC toolpaths.
- Variable rounds are difficult to manufacture. Consider the necessity of this feature as you are creating your model.

Always consider the order in which features are going to be manufactured. The order of round and draft creation can affect the resulting geometry and should be added as late as possible in the feature order. For example, draft geometry should be added to the model before rounds. Consider the order in which rounds are added to the model as well and how their order affects the geometry and each other.

Suppressing by layer provides an easy method of suppressing groups of features.

You can set rounds and drafts to be automatically added to layers for easy suppression using the Options dialog box (*File* tab **> Options > Configuration Editor)**. The **def_layer Configuration File** option has a value for both rounds (layer_round_feat) and drafts (layer_draft_feat*)*. Enter a name for the round or draft after the value, separated by a space (e.g., layer_draft_feat drafts). Once either of these features are added to the model, the layer displays in the model. All subsequent rounds or drafts added to the model are automatically added to the respective layer. To suppress the layer, display the layer tree in the Navigator window. Select the layer, right-click, and select **Select Items** to select all of the layer items. Select the *Model* tab and select **Operations > Suppress > Suppress** to suppress the selected items.

23.3 Model Investigation

Modify an existing model using the investigation tools.

You cannot always create new models. In many cases, you are required to continue someone else's design or make modifications to a previously completed model. In these cases, you should always investigate the model to review it. Some reviewing techniques that can be used include the following:

- Model player
- Model tree
- Relations
- Info options

Model Player

The model player (*Tools* tab and click ![icon] (Model Player)) enables you to review the construction history of a model, one feature at a time. This technique is especially useful when working with models created by other modelers. Using the model player can give you an idea of the modeler's design intent and modeling techniques.

Model Tree

The model tree displays the model's features and can be used to review the model. It can also be customized to display additional information using the Model Tree Items and Model Tree Columns dialog boxes, as shown in Figure 23–1 and Figure 23–2, respectively.

To open the Model Tree Items dialog box, click

![icon] *and select **Tree Filters**. The **Suppressed Objects** option enables you to either remove or display suppressed features in the model tree.*

Figure 23–1

To open the Model Tree Items dialog box, click

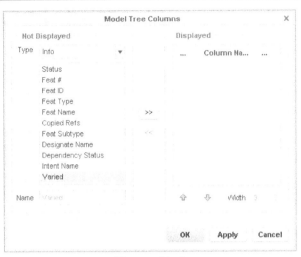

🛠️ ▼ *and select Tree Columns.*

Figure 23–2

Info Options

The Investigate group in the *Tools* tab contains a number of options that can be used to investigate the model. These options include **Feature**, **Feature List**, **Model**, and **Reference Viewer**. You can also right-click and select the **Info** flyout menu to obtain some of the information options.

Relation Information

Relations are used in models to control design intent. To investigate existing relations in a model, use any of the following methods:

- Select the *Tools* tab and click d= (Relations). Any relations that exist in the model display in the Relations dialog box. Relation comment statements (if added) help you to understand the intent of the relation. You can also click |↤↦| in the Relations dialog box to highlight the dimensions that are affected by the relation.

- Click 🗂️ (Feature) in the *Tools* tab and select the feature. Any relations that exist in the feature display at the bottom of the Browser window in the *Relation Table* area.

- Select the *Tools* tab > **Model Intent** > **Relations and Parameters** to open the Browser window that displays all of the relations that exist in the model.

23.4 Interactive Exercise

 Create a flexible model that communicates the design intent.

The model shown in Figure 23–3 must be designed so that the changes shown in Figure 23–3 and Figure 23–4 are possible. Consider the following issues:

- Types of features to be used.
- Best feature order.
- Dimension scheme.

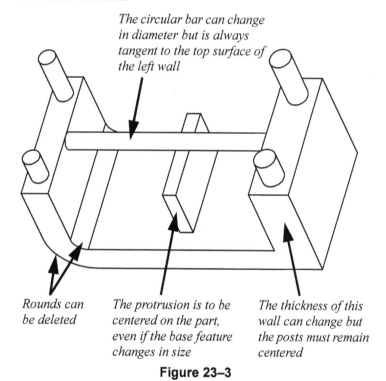

The circular bar can change in diameter but is always tangent to the top surface of the left wall

Rounds can be deleted

The protrusion is to be centered on the part, even if the base feature changes in size

The thickness of this wall can change but the posts must remain centered

Figure 23–3

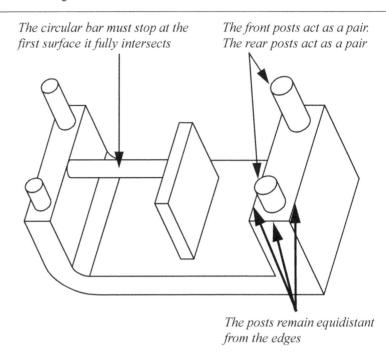

The circular bar must stop at the first surface it fully intersects

The front posts act as a pair. The rear posts act as a pair

The posts remain equidistant from the edges

Figure 23–4

Appendix A

Additional Exercises

This appendix contains additional exercises to practice some of the functionality covered in this training guide. The exercises can be done during class if time permits or they on your own time as they do not require pre-existing files.

Exercise A1 | Creating Parts

 Create new parts and use the appropriate tools to create the geometry.

Goal | After you complete this exercise, you will be able to:

✓ **Create geometry**

Task 1 - Create new parts.

1. Set the working directory to the *Appendix A* folder.

2. Create the new part shown in Figure A–1, using the default template.

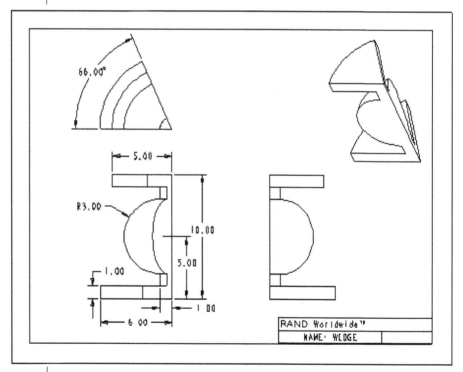

Figure A–1

3. Create the new part shown in Figure A–2, using the default template.

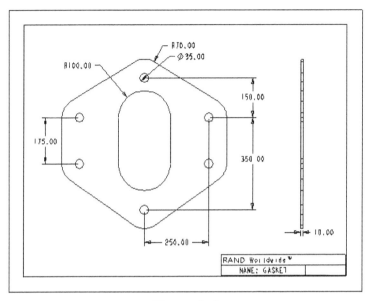

Figure A–2

4. Create the new part shown in Figure A–3, using the default template.

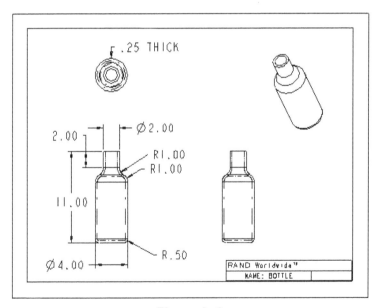

Figure A–3

Exercise A2 | Sketched Features

 Create a new part and use the extrude feature to create the base and secondary features.

Goal | After you complete this exercise, you will be able to:

✓ **Sketch features**

Task 1 - Create a new part.

---

1. Set the working directory to the *Appendix A* folder.

2. Create the new part shown in Figure A–4, using the default template.

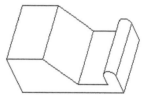

Figure A–4

Task 2 - Create protrusions.

---

1. Create the D-shaped and slanted protrusions shown in Figure A–5. For the slanted protrusion use an open section and ensure that the height of the protrusion is not beyond the point at which the slanted surface and vertical surface intersect (the feature fails if this occurs).

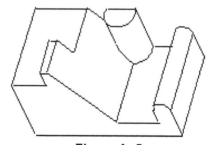

Figure A–5

Exercise A3 | Sketched Geometry

 Create new parts and use the appropriate tools to create the geometry.

Goal

After you complete this exercise, you will be able to:

✓ **Sketch geometry**

Task 1 - Create the following parts.

1. Set the working directory to the *Appendix A* folder.

2. Create the new parts shown in Figure A–6, Figure A–7, Figure A–8, and Figure A–9, using the default template. The dimensions of these parts have been omitted to help you understand that Creo Parametric is a design tool. Once the model has been built, dimensions can be modified to their required values. Build the parts, keeping in mind your design intent for the model.

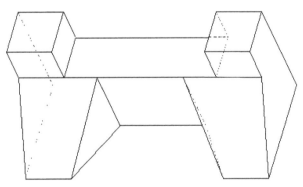

Figure A–6

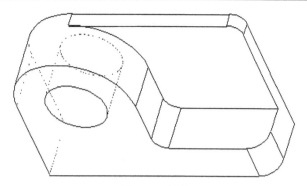

Figure A–7

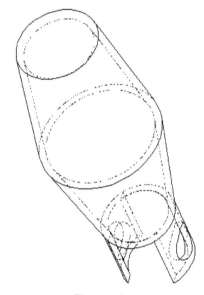

Figure A–8

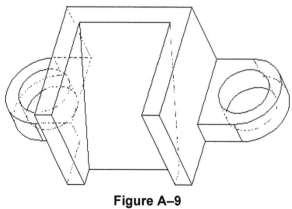

Figure A–9

Exercise A4 | Feature Creation

 Create a new part and the geometry.

 Create new part and ask question to ensure the geometry meets the design intent.

Goal | After you complete this exercise, you will be able to:

✓ **Create a part by recognizing the required features and duplication techniques**

Task 1 - Create a new part.

1. Set the working directory to the *Appendix A* folder.

2. Create a new part called [hubguard], as shown in Figure A–10, using the default template. Create the protrusion so that the default view is as shown in the upper right corner in Figure A–10.

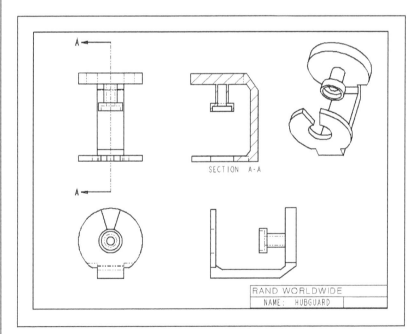

Figure A–10

3. Save the part and close the window.

Task 2 - Create a new part.

1. Create the new part called [chamfer.prt] as shown in Figure A–11, using the default template. Consider the following design intent suggestions when creating parent-child relationships:

    - Should the holes be revolved sketched cuts or holes?
    - Should the holes be created as individual features?
    - Is there an easy duplication technique that can be used to ensure that all holes are dependent on one another?

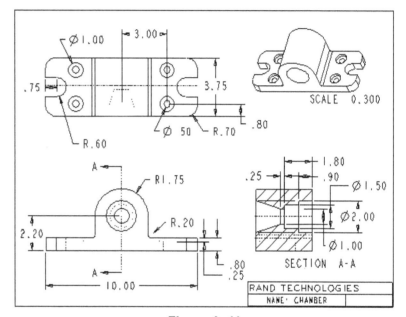

Figure A–11

2. Save the model and close the window.

Exercise A5 | Connector

 Edit the part and fix the failed features using either method.

In this exercise, you will resolve feature failures with limited instructions. You will then modify the part to make it more robust and flexible to design changes. To resolve the failure you can use either method. Note that if you intend to use Resolve mode, the config option must be set to **resolve_mode.**

Goal

After you complete this exercise, you will be able to:

✓ **Resolve the failure with limited instructions**

Task 1 - Open a part file.

1. Set the working directory to the *Appendix A* folder.

2. Open **connector.prt**. The model displays as shown in Figure A–12.

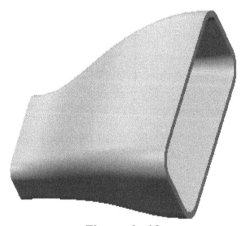

Figure A–12

Task 2 - Implement a design change.

In this task, you will implement a design change request. The total length of the connector part is 2. The design change calls for a 0.125 change to make the overall length 2.125. The overall length is controlled by a datum plane named CONNECTOR_LENGTH.

1. Edit the CONNECTOR_LENGTH datum plane and change the offset value from 2 to [2.125], as shown in Figure A–13.

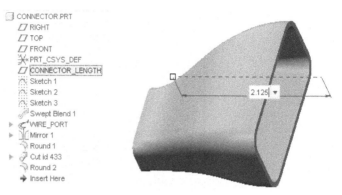

Figure A–13

2. Regenerate the part.

Hint: Remove the edge references that no longer exist.

3. Resolve the feature that fails.

4. Edit the depth of Cut id 433 to [.625].

Task 3 - Modify the part to make it more robust.

1. Once the feature failure has been resolved and the part has successfully regenerated, make the required changes so that the original references for Round 3 can be added, as shown in Figure A–14.

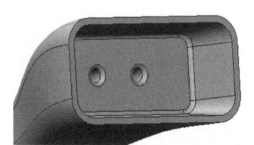

Figure A–14

2. Save the part and erase it from memory.

Exercise A6 | Drawing Templates

 Create a new drawing and use the appropriate tools to create a drawing template.

 Create a drawing using the new template.

In this exercise, you will create a drawing template with three views. To complete the exercise, you will use this template to create a drawing. Figure A–15 shows the final template that you will be creating.

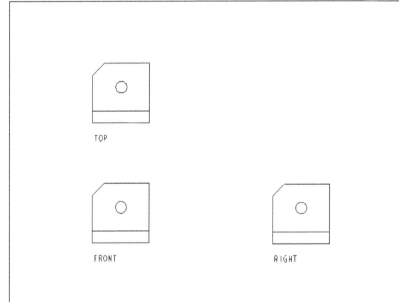

Figure A–15

Goal | After you complete this exercise, you will be able to:

- ✓ **Create a drawing template**
- ✓ **Use a template to create a drawing**

Task 1 - Create a drawing template.

1. Select **File > New > Drawing**.

2. For the name, enter [template].

3. Clear the **Use default template** option.

4. Specify the drawing template as **Empty**, the Orientation as **Landscape**, and the size as **C**.

Task 2 - Enable the template application.

---

1. Select the *Tools* tab and click ▱ (Template) in the Applications group.

Task 3 - Place the first General view in the template.

---

1. Select the *Layout* tab. Click ▱ (Template View).

2. The Template View Instructions dialog box opens. It enables you to define the attributes of each view in the template.

3. For the View Name, enter [Front].

4. For the View Orientation, accept the default of **General**.

5. Click ⬚ Place View... ⬚ and place the template view in the lower left corner of the drawing, as shown in Figure A–15. When placing the view symbol for the general view, you can select between two methods:

   • Select a view symbol location. Drawing views created using this method have their scale tied to the global drawing scale.

The second method is only available for general views,. Projection views inherit the specification of the bounding box from their parent general view.

   • Click the left mouse button, draw a view bounding box, and release the left mouse button. The intent of the bounding box is to enable Creo Parametric 1.0 to fill a specific area on the drawing with the model view. Drawing views created using this method have their own scale independent of the global drawing scale.

Task 4 - Place projected views in the template.

---

1. Click ⬚ New ⬚ to start a new template view.

2. For the name of the view, enter [Top].

3. For the View Orientation, select **Projection**.

4. Click _____ Place... _____ and place the view template in the top left corner of the drawing, as shown in Figure A–15.

5. Click _____ New _____ to start a new template view.

6. For the name of the view, enter [Right] and for the View Orientation, select **Projection**. Place the view in the right bottom corner of the drawing, as shown in Figure A–15.

7. Close the dialog box.

8. Save the template and close the window.

Task 5 - Create a drawing using the newly created template.

For the view to automatically display as shown in the template, the model must have FRONT as a saved view.

1. Create a new drawing using the new template. The template is stored in the current working directory. Create the drawing using any of the models in the current working directory.

2. Save the drawing and close the window.

Appendix B

Additional Exercises

This appendix contains additional exercises for practicing some of the functionality covered in this training guide. The exercises can be done during the class if time permits, or on your own time as they do not require pre-existing files.

Exercise B1 | Place a Section

 Create a sketch and reuse the sketch to create the geometry using the **File Import** command.

Goal | After you complete this exercise, you will be able to:

✓ **Place saved sections in a sketch**

Task 1 - Create a new part.

1. Set the working directory to the *Appendix B* folder.

2. Create a new part using the default template.

3. Sketch the extruded base feature of the part shown in Figure B–1 on the default datum planes. When the sketch has regenerated successfully, save it.

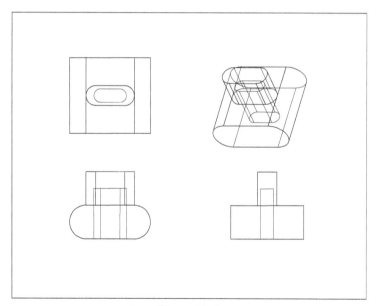

Figure B–1

You can also use the Copy and Paste options.

4. Use the saved sketch to create two additional features, by clicking ⬚ (File System) in the Get Data group.

5. Save the model and erase it from memory.

Exercise B2 | Advanced Geometry

 Create text using the *Sketch* tab.

In this exercise, you will create the part shown in Figure B–2.

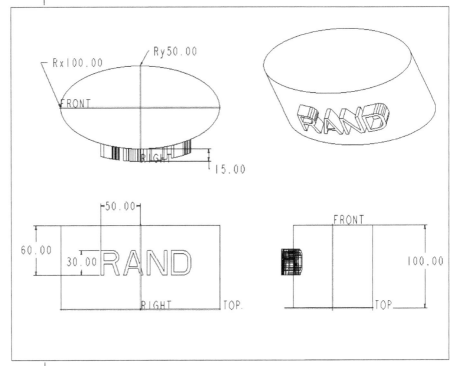

Figure B–2

Goal | After you complete this exercise, you will be able to:

✓ **Sketch text**

Task 1 - Create a new part.

1. Set the working directory to the *Appendix B* folder.

2. Create a new part using the default template.

3. Create the base extruded protrusion by sketching the ellipse on the default datum planes, as shown in Figure B–2.

4. Create another extruded protrusion. Select datum plane **FRONT** as the sketching plane. Use 🄰 (Text) to sketch the text [RAND]. Extrude the text using a **Blind** depth of [75]. This is an arbitrary value to be cut away in the next step.

5. Create a cut to trim the text. Sketch the cut on datum plane TOP.

   In Sketcher mode, use ⌷ (Offset) to create a cut that follows the outline of the base protrusion at an offset of [15], as shown in Figure B–2. Extrude the cut through all.

Exercise B3 | Sweeps

 Create sweep features using the appropriate options.

Goal | After you complete this exercise, you will be able to:

✓ **Create swept features**

Task 1 - Create new parts.

1. Set the working directory to the *Appendix B* folder.

2. Create the parts shown in Figure B–3 and Figure B–4, using swept features where needed.

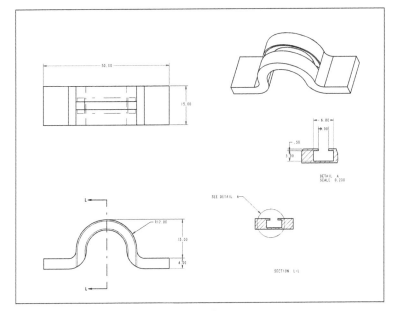

Figure B–3

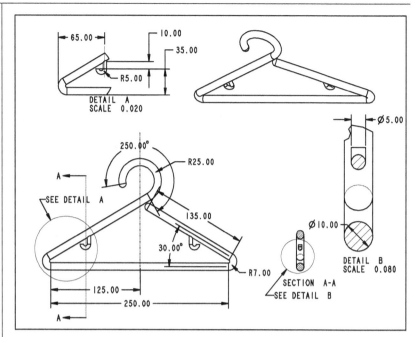

Figure B–4

3. Save the models and erase them from memory.

Exercise B4	# Create Blend Features

 Create a blend feature using the appropriate options.

In this exercise, you will create the blend feature shown in Figure B–5. This model requires the creation of seven sub-sections, the first of which is a sketcher point.

Figure B–5

Goal

After you complete this exercise, you will be able to:

- ✓ **Create blended features**
- ✓ **Add a sketcher point as a sub-section**
- ✓ **Edit the definition of the blend**

Task 1 - Create a new part.

---

1. Set the working directory to the *Appendix B* folder.

2. Create a part called [bowling_pin] using the default template.

Task 2 - Create a Blend feature.

---

1. Select **Shapes > Blend** in the *Model* tab.

2. Create a Straight blend.

3. Select datum plane **TOP** as the sketching plane and accept the direction for the blend feature.

---

4. Select **Right** as the orientation direction and select datum plane **RIGHT** as the reference.

5. Sketch each section as a circular entity located at the intersection of datum planes FRONT and RIGHT. Use the diameter values shown in Table B–1 to create sub-sections.

Table B–1

Sub-Section	Diameter
1	1.75
2	2.00
3	2.50
4	1.00
5	1.50
6	0.25

6. For the last section, click ✳ to create a sketcher point. Place the point at the intersection of datum planes FRONT and RIGHT.

7. Enter the depth values for each section when prompted, as shown in Table B–2.

Table B–2

Sub-Section	Depth
2	0.5
3	3.0
4	3.0
5	2.0
6	1.0
7	0.1

8. Complete the blend. The model displays as shown in Figure B–6.

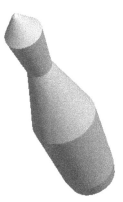

Figure B–6

Task 3 - Edit the definition of the blend.

1. Select the feature, right-click, and select **Edit Definition**. The Blend dialog box opens.

2. Change the blend to *Smooth*.

3. Complete the feature. The model displays as shown in Figure B–7.

Figure B–7

4. Select the feature, right-click, and select **Edit**. All dimensions that were used to create the model display. Modify some of the values to change the size and depth of the sections.

5. Save the model and erase it from memory.

Exercise B5 | Rotational Patterns

 Create a pattern using the appropriate pattern options.

Goal

After you complete this exercise, you will be able to:

✓ **Create rotational patterns as shown in Figure B–8**

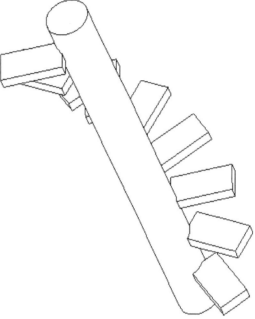

Figure B–8

Task 1 - Create a new part.

In this task you will create a new part using the default template. Create the base extruded protrusion as a circular section with a diameter of [2]. Extrude the feature to a blind depth of [20].

Task 2 - Create a rectangular extruded protrusion.

In this task you will create a rectangular extruded protrusion to be patterned as shown in Figure B–8. The pattern must be driven by both a linear dimension and an angular dimension. To accomplish this, you will create datums on the fly for both the sketch and orientation planes. For the sketching references, only select the axis of the cylinder and the datum on the fly that you created as the orientation plane. DO NOT select the cylinder as the reference.

Task 3 - Pattern the rectangular protrusion.

In this task you will pattern the rectangular protrusion. Select the linear dimension that was used to create the first datum on the fly (sketching plane), as the first dimension to drive the pattern. Select the angular dimension that was used to create the second datum on the fly (orientation plane) as the second dimension in the first direction to drive the pattern.

Exercise B6 | Axial Patterns

 Create an axial pattern to create the cuts.

In this exercise, you will create a radial pattern of an extruded cut. You use an Axis pattern to create the required rotational pattern. The model shown on the left in Figure B–9 represents the original model. Once the cut is created and patterned and the pattern is modified, the model displays as shown on the right in Figure B–9.

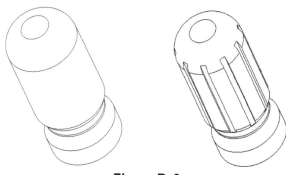

Figure B–9

Goal | After you complete this exercise, you will be able to:

✓ **Create features that can be patterned radially**
✓ **Create radial patterns**

Task 1 - Create a new part.

1. Set the working directory to the *Appendix B* folder.

2. Create a part called [switch.prt] using the default template.

3. Sketch the section on the default datum planes as shown in Figure B–10, and create the revolved protrusion.

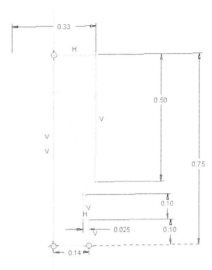

Figure B–10

Task 2 - Create the rounds.

1. Create the rounds shown in Figure B–11.

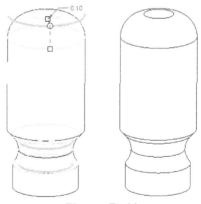

Figure B–11

Task 3 - Create the cut feature to be patterned radially.

1. Click ☐ (Extrude) to create an extruded feature. The *Extrude* tab displays.

Alternatively, you can click
Define...
in the
Placement slide-up panel
to access Sketcher mode.

2. Select the top surface of the switch as the sketching plane as shown in Figure B–12.

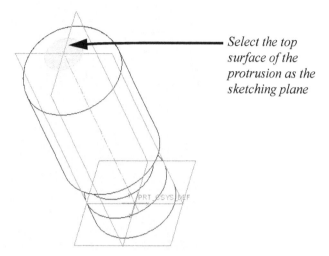

Select the top surface of the protrusion as the sketching plane

Figure B–12

3. Click 🔲 to open the References dialog box.

4. Select datum plane **RIGHT** and the outside surface of the revolved protrusion as references, as shown in Figure B–13.

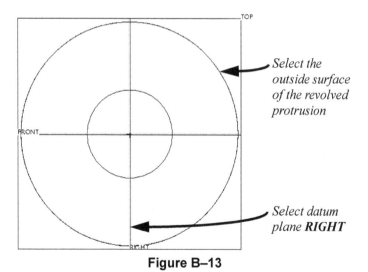

Select the outside surface of the revolved protrusion

Select datum plane RIGHT

Figure B–13

5. Close the References dialog box.

6. Sketch the section shown in Figure B–14.

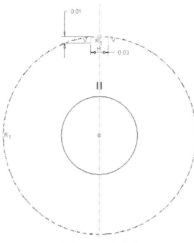

Figure B–14

7. Complete the sketch.

8. Set the **Depth** option to extrude to the next surface using ⌸.

9. Click ⟋ to set this extruded feature to remove material. Click ⟋ (the one on the left) to flip the direction of the feature creation, if necessary. Hover your cursor over the icon to display a short help line in the message window.

10. Complete the feature. The model displays as shown in Figure B–15.

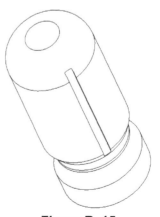

Figure B–15

Task 4 - Radially pattern the extrusion.

1. Select the extruded feature that was just created and click
   ⊞ (Pattern).

2. In the Pattern Type drop-down list, select **Axis**.

3. For the axis reference to pattern about, select **axis A_2**.

4. For the number of instances in the first direction, enter [20] as
   shown in Figure B–16.

5. For the pattern increment for the first direction, enter [18] as shown
   in Figure B–16.

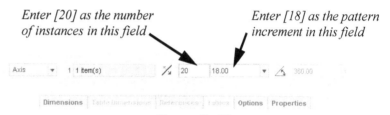

Enter [20] as the number of instances in this field   *Enter [18] as the pattern increment in this field*

Figure B–16

6. Complete the pattern. The model displays as shown in
   Figure B–17.

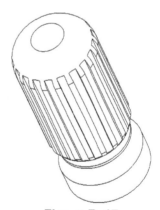

Figure B–17

Task 5 - Modify the pattern.

1. Select the pattern that was just created, right-click, and select
   Edit. All of the dimensions associated with the patterned feature
   display.

2. Double-click on the 20 Extrudes dimension. For the new number of cuts, enter [10] and press <Enter>.

3. Regenerate the model. It displays as shown in Figure B–18. Note how the pattern does not update to equally space the cuts around the entire diameter of the model.

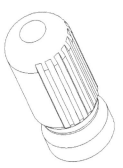

Figure B–18

4. Select the pattern, right-click, and select **Edit Definition**. The tab displays.

5. Click 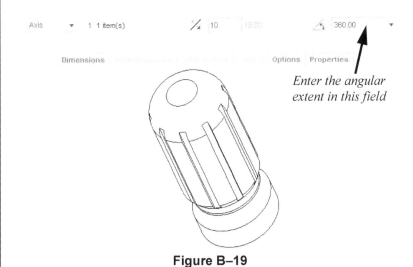 next to the *Angular increment* collector (i.e., the 18 value) for the first direction. The tab updates as shown in Figure B–19. Complete the pattern. The model updates because the system has been set to automatically space the number of instances equally, based on the angular extent that is set in the field.

| Axis | ▼ | 1 1 item(s) | | 10 | 13.00 | | 360.00 | ▼ |

Enter the angular extent in this field

Dimensions   Options Properties

Figure B–19

6. Save the model and erase it from memory.

Exercise B7 | Part and Assembly Creation

 Create and assemble the new parts.

Goal

After you complete this exercise, you will be able to:

✓ **Create a part**
✓ **Create an assembly**

Task 1 - Create the parts.

In this task you will create the parts that are used during the assembly task as shown in Figure B–20, Figure B–21, Figure B–22, Figure B–23, and Figure B–24.

At the end of this exercise, there are tips on creating each part. Try to refer to them only if necessary.

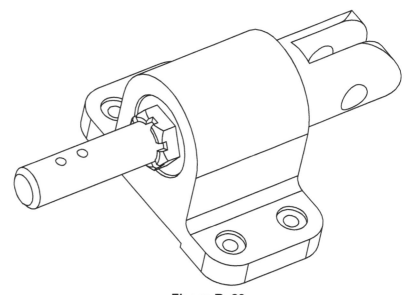

Figure B–20

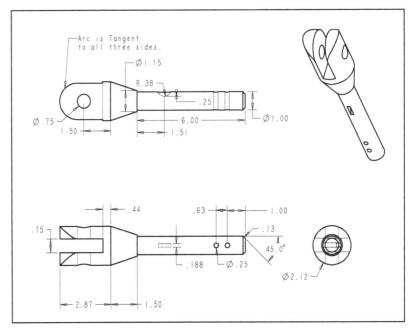

Figure B–21 Yoke

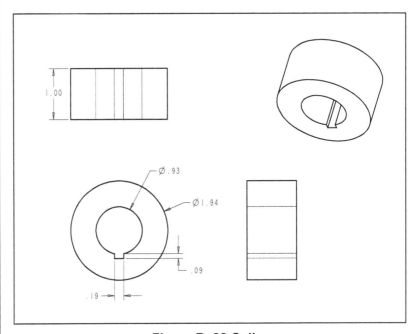

Figure B–22 Collar

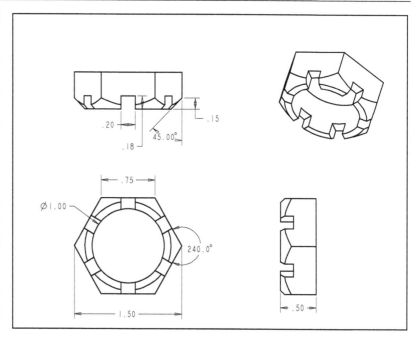

Figure B–23 Nut

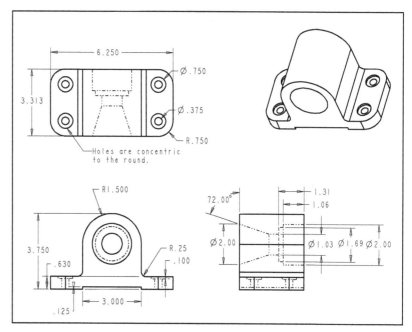

Figure B–24 Base

Task 2 - Create the assembly.

In this task you will create an assembly that should enable the yoke, collar, and nut to be rotated as shown in Figure B–25 and Figure B–26. Check for interference between the components.

Hint: The sloped surfaced on the yoke can be used to mate to the base.

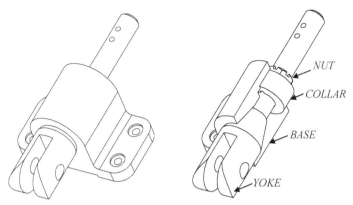

Figure B–25

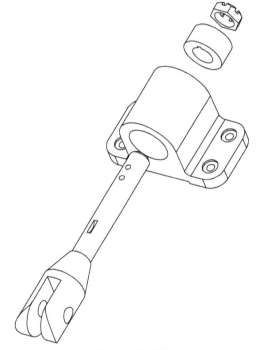

Figure B–26

YOKE

1. Create the model using the default template.

2. Revolve a base feature (the sketch must be closed and a centerline is required as an axis of revolution). Exaggerate the small step where the sloped surface meets the shaft portion; this might eliminate regeneration errors. After a successful regeneration, modify it to the proper value.

3. To create outside diameter dimensions, the following selections are required:

   - Select the edge/endpoint.
   - Select the centerline (required for the axis of revolution).
   - Select the edge/endpoint once again.
   - Place the dimension.

4. Create the large arc cut on both sides of a center datum using the **Through All** depth option. To create a tangent arc to three sides, sketch centerlines on each of the sides and align them with the part. Then sketch a 3-tangent arc and align the endpoints to the part. The arc is assumed to be tangent to the centerlines (which are aligned to the part).

5. Create the small arc cut on both sides of a center datum using the **Blind** depth option. Use a 3-Point arc to sketch the shape. Align the endpoints.

6. Create a 45 x D Edge chamfer on the bottom of the shaft.

7. Create the large hole. Use a Linear hole placed on the center datum dimensioned from the edge and aligned to a center datum. When making the screen selection to locate the hole, select a spot very close to the center datum. The system then enables you to align the hole to the center datum when the center datum is selected as a reference. If the screen selection is not close enough, the alignment prompt is not given, but 0 can be entered as the dimension.

8. Create a small hole similar to Step 7 and pattern the second small hole.

BASE

1. Create the model using the default template.

2. Extrude a base feature on both sides of default datum planes. Sketch the feature so that it is centered on a datum plane (the arc center can then be aligned to the datum). Do not add rounds to the base feature; add them as a separate round feature.

3. Revolve a cut for the hole in the boss.

4. Create the four corner rounds.

5. Create a counterbore hole by placing two coaxial holes on a datum axis. Create a datum axis using the round, it is considered to be cylinder. Copy and mirror the coaxial holes.

6. Create the two edge rounds on the boss.

COLLAR

1. Create the model using the default template.

2. Extrude or revolve a base feature centered on default datum planes.

3. Create a cut.

NUT

1. Create the model using the default template.

2. Extrude a base feature centered on default datum planes. Sketch and regenerate half the sketch, then mirror to complete the sketch.

3. Create the sloped edge by revolving a cut.

Create the square cut and pattern it. This option expands on dimension patterns so that you can simply select the patterning direction. Because you no longer need to select a dimension directly from the pattern leader, this pattern type can help you pattern features that do not explicitly have a dimension for the required pattern.

Appendix C

Suggested Steps for Exercise in Chapter 23

Exercise C1 | Suggested Steps for Exercise Chapter 23

There are numerous ways that this model can be built and dimensioned to incorporate the required design intent. The following steps are an example of one way to do it. The dimension values shown were selected arbitrarily.

1. Create the model using the default template.

2. Sketch and locate the base feature on both sides of datum plane FRONT, as shown in Figure C–1. The section was dimensioned this way to enable the width of the right sidewall to be modified independent of the other areas. A vertical centerline is used to maintain symmetry of the part about datum plane RIGHT.

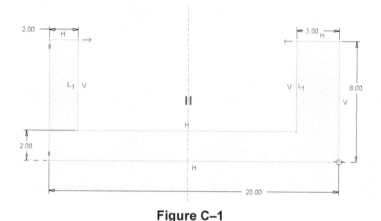

Figure C–1

3. Extrude to a depth of [10], as shown in Figure C–2.

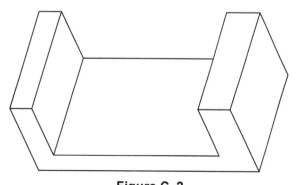

Figure C–2

4. Create rounds on the edges of the lower left corner as shown in Figure C–3. The rounds were not sketched as fillet arcs in the section of the base feature. Therefore, that they can be easily deleted, if necessary.

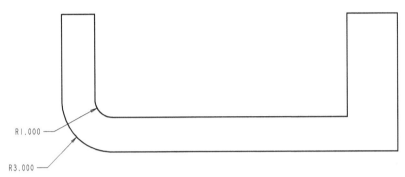

RI.000

R3.000

Figure C–3

5. Create the first protrusion on the right side. Select the references shown in Figure C–4, and sketch a construction circle so that it is tangent with the three references. Sketch a concentric circle referencing the construction circle. The protrusion remains centered on the top of the wall and equidistant from the edges.

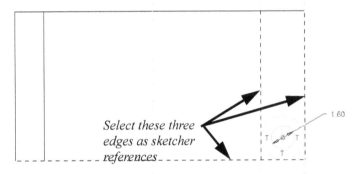

Select these three edges as sketcher references

1.60

Figure C–4

6. Extrude the protrusion to a blind depth of [2.0], as shown in Figure C–5. The technique of using the construction circle keeps the protrusion centered on the top of the wall no matter what the width happens to be. Test or *flex* the model to see if this is true, as shown in Figure C–6.

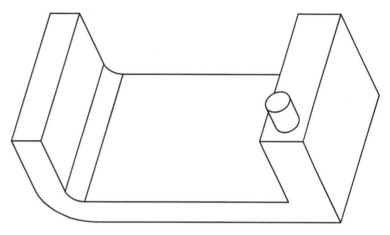

Figure C–5

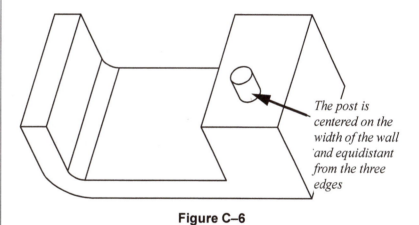

The post is centered on the width of the wall and equidistant from the three edges

Figure C–6

7. Create the front protrusion on the left side, as shown in Figure C–7. Being centered on the wall was not a criterion for this side, so a different dimensioning scheme can be used, if required. Select **A_1** as a reference so that the two protrusions are aligned with one another. The height of the protrusion must always be the same as that of the front protrusion on the right side. To accomplish this, use the **To Selected** option when specifying the depth and select the top surface of the front, right protrusion. When the height of the front right protrusion is modified, the front left protrusion also updates.

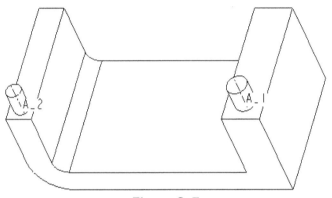

Figure C–7

8. Create the rear protrusions by selecting the two front protrusions and using 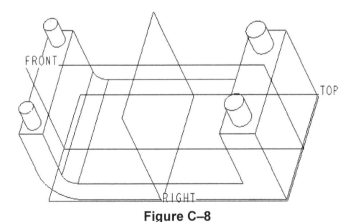, as shown in Figure C–8. For the mirroring plane, select datum plane **FRONT**. The rear protrusions can be modified independent of the front protrusions, if you open the Options slide-up panel in the Mirror dashboard and clear the checkmark in front of the **Copy as dependent** option. Remember, clearing the **Copy as dependent** option cannot be undone.

Figure C–8

9. Create the protrusion in the center of the part, as shown in Figure C–9 and Figure C–10. To keep it centered on the part, sketch on both sides of datum plane FRONT. Use a centerline to keep the section symmetric about datum plane RIGHT. Extrude the protrusion to a blind depth of [7.0].

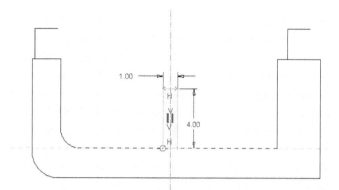

Figure C–9

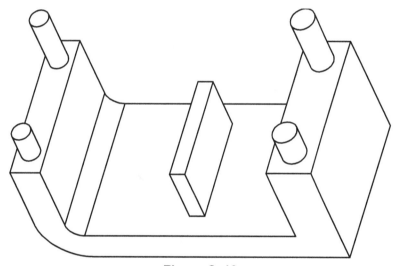

Figure C–10

10. Create the circular protrusion shown in Figure C–11 and Figure C–12. It must remain tangent to the top of the wall on the left side. Its depth must be defined so that it stops at the first surface it fully intersects. Therefore, you need to use the **To Next** option.

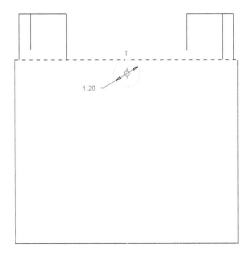

Figure C–11

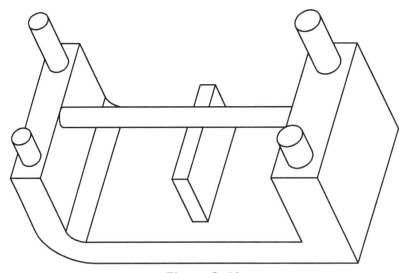

Figure C–12

11. Modify the height of the center protrusion so that the circular protrusion fully intersects it, as shown in Figure C–13. What would happen if the circular protrusion had been created before the square protrusion?

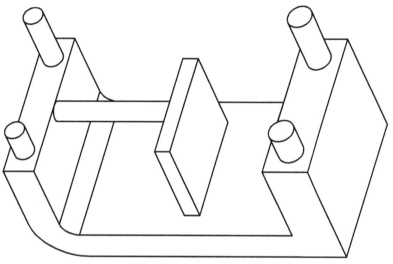

Figure C–13

12. Fully *flex* the model to ensure that all of the design criteria have been incorporated.

www.ingramcontent.com/pod-product-compliance
Lightning Source LLC
Chambersburg PA
CBHW080145060326
40689CB00018B/3853